HOW YOU LEAVE THEM FEELING

HOW YOU LEAVE THEM FEELING

Your Foundation for Inspiring Love & Relationships

LISA FERRELL & JESSE FERRELL

For permission requests, write to the publisher, addressed "Attention: Permissions Coordinator," at the address below.

Publish Your Purpose
141 Weston Street, #155
Hartford, CT, 06141

The opinions expressed by the Author are not necessarily those held by Publish Your Purpose.

Ordering Information: Quantity sales and special discounts are available on quantity purchases by corporations, associations, and others. For details, contact the publisher at hello@publishyourpurpose.com.

Edited by: Lori McFerran, Laura Kaiser, August Li, Jenni Murphy, Cher Weldon
Cover design by: Cornelia Murariu, Jesse Ferrell
Photography by: Julie LeGrand-Lebauza
Typeset by: Medlar Publishing Solutions Pvt Ltd., India

Printed in the United States of America.

ISBN: 978-1-955985-88-8 (hardcover)
ISBN: 978-1-955985-90-1 (eBook)

Library of Congress Control Number: 2022914689

First edition, January 2023.

The information contained within this book is strictly for informational purposes. The material may include information, products, or services by third parties. As such, the Author and Publisher do not assume responsibility or liability for any third-party material or opinions. The publisher is not responsible for websites (or their content) that are not owned by the publisher. Readers are advised to do their own due diligence when it comes to making decisions.

The mission of Publish Your Purpose is to discover and publish authors who are striving to make a difference in the world. We give underrepresented voices power and a stage to share their stories, speak their truth, and impact their communities. Do you have a book idea you would like us to consider publishing? Please visit PublishYourPurpose.com for more information.

Table of Contents

Foreword

There are limitless disciplines offering the opportunity to team up with trusted advisers in order to help develop and maintain happiness in your most important relationships! I have spent countless years in serving others through my educational and professional masteries. I cherish the feelings stored within me after teaming up with individuals, couples, families, and organizations in order to help them improve not only the best attributes of their relationships, but also enhance the quality of their lives.

That is exactly what you will gain by reading and putting into practice the ideas and concepts shared within this book. Remain open to receive the opportunity for advancing the quality of your relationships and to adopt excellent life improvement principles. Lisa and Jesse Ferrell have profoundly discovered their true life calling by continuing to advance and share their universal life concept of How You Leave Them Feeling and how embracing this concept can serve you well.

This book focuses on sharing the foundation of love and relationships, offering a very simple yet attractive roadmap for your success in developing and maintaining the best spirit in all of your important relationships.

You will likely encounter ideas and concepts within this book that you are already familiar with. Remain open to tie those ideas and concepts together with the newly shared ideas. You will move through chapters focusing on trusting your gut instincts, building relationship equity, creating unbreakable relationships, and more.

I highly recommend that you move beyond just consuming the knowledge from this book. Be mindful of how to put the authors' recommended action steps into practice as you seek to navigate through the minefields of life while embracing and forever adding love and care in your relationships that matter most to you.

Janice Sheree Hunter
Marriage & Family Therapist

Introduction: Setting the Stage

This book is intended to be a breath of fresh air and solution-based intelligence that helps you move from feeling like you have one foot in the grave to soaring to amazing new heights with yourself and all of your important relationships.

* * *

As we sit at the beautiful Siena Golf Club located west of the Las Vegas Strip, the atmosphere captures the tranquility of abundance with luscious green palm trees stretching twenty feet in the air. Imagine yourself sitting in this private VIP location surrounded by breathtaking waterfalls and lakes. You feel a spirit of calm and tranquility.

You can't get away from the magnetizing inner peace pulling you into the escape through the lush rolling green peaks and valleys populating the scenery. The color green represents the color of life, renewal, nature, and energy, and its meaning is associated with growth, harmony, freshness, safety, fertility, and environment.

Just as a serene landscape can elicit a sense of inner peace, we have loaded this book with nuggets of experience and truth that can help develop the energy and harmony in you that will attract your best connections. In that sense, these writings are an analogy for the pursuit of tranquility and growth.

This is especially important now, as we are living through new and often scary and unprecedented times. Our entire world is being impacted by a serious global pandemic. As a result, people have lost touch with the foundation and basics of how to develop and maintain healthy relationships with self and others.

Most relationships involve a degree of confrontation and conflict. It's likely that you will argue more during difficult and stressful times. You may start worrying about your mental health and the health of your loved ones. Or, you may be facing the unknown and increased relationship tension and financial uncertainty. These are heavy matters to carry around with you, clouding your mind with unresolved negative baggage. All of the classic marital stressors have been amplified by the impact of the pandemic.

It goes beyond merely practicing bad habits that are destructive to your important relationships. Additionally, much of our world is reverberating from extended periods of social isolation. People are feeling increased levels of anxiety, and countless relationships have been negatively affected by spending twenty-four hours per day, seven days per week with the entire immediate family.

It's possible that this intermittent world shutdown and pandemic offer brighter hopes, prompting refocusing on your roles, values, and on what really matters most.

The purpose of this book is to create a counterbalance in the current wave of negativity, fear, and disruption in businesses, professions, and home life. Our number one goal is to help you build a solid foundation for inspiring love and relationships during these challenging times as well as during ordinary times.

How did we learn how to do this? Our knowledge comes from our experience as professional life coaches and the many inspirational leadership speaking engagements in which we have participated. When we are asked what we do for a living, we respond by saying that we make a life and a living by helping to free others from their concerns.

The inspiration to write the first book in what we hope will become a How You Leave Them Feeling series came from a powerful executive coaching session. It was clear that our senior executive client was failing to realize that how he left his key team members feeling was hurting his business and squashing opportunities. His team was hemorrhaging from his negative communication style. Even with the high level of intelligence of this senior executive, the notion of focusing on the importance of how he was leaving others feeling had escaped him.

What he had not yet discovered was that choosing to care about self and others is a magical connection to the How You Leave Them Feeling concept. Focusing on how you leave yourself and others feeling is what will allow you to build connections with others and with yourself. One of the best ways to leave people feeling is to leave them wanting more! When you leave others wanting more of you, it extends the relationship to greater depths.

Lisa and I want our first coauthored book to help bring solutions and hopeful measures back to the lives of people we may never meet. We have chosen to write this book together from our diverse and overlapping perspectives so that you will encounter the full range of our combined experienced voices throughout this read. In an effort to guide and stimulate you toward attracting and nurturing healthy relationships, we will share sensitive and provocative intimate details about our own unique relationship and marriage.

We are asking you to allow our book to be a guide for how to maintain healthy relationships that can survive normal, day-to-day life and sustain themselves even during a crisis.

Regardless of whether you are moving from how to build sustainable great love and relationships with others or you're simply seeking to move from good to great in your relationships, the following pages will propose useful, practical, simple options to elevate the quality of your relationships. Your situation may be more like moving from okay to good or good to great! Either way, our book may be used as a foundation for building and sustaining meaningful and gratifying relationships.

The past twenty-one years have been a blink and the treasured stories and life coaching solutions we offer will be life-changing opportunities for you or those with whom you choose to share our book. We hope to inspire you to move from pushing to be right to choosing to consistently do what is right to fuel all of your important relationships.

While reading this book, you will find passages that mirror emotions, feelings, and actions that you have experienced, displayed, or responded to throughout the years. You will also likely find new concepts and offerings. They will invite you to practice new and proven love and relationship-actionable concepts based on real-life experiences, offering tested truths that consistently bring value to your relationships. This is the perfect time for us to applaud you for choosing to read this book. Whether you are seeking to gain nuggets of wisdom for yourself or your loved ones, congratulations are in order.

With advanced permission from our amazing personal and professional coaching clients and inspirational speaking audiences, we will be using great case studies to help you understand the power of building relationship equity with yourself first.

After you have used the foundation of building relationship equity with yourself, we recommend that you use this principle to fuel and rebuild all your relationships. Buckle up, let's go for a ride!

* * *

Chapter 1

Living Life by Design

Living life by design was discovered while listening to one of our favorite and very important coaching clients, Tammy Harrison, complain about her dreadful life matters. Tammy spent twenty years climbing the professional ladder leading up to directing a staff of one hundred and sixty frontline workers in the hospitality industry. She was proud of her hotel administration degree and remained hopeful that gaining this level of education outside of her day job would give her some type of professional advantage. After listening to a thirty-five-minute rant, it was clear that she was simply waiting for things to happen in her favor without applying any intentional action steps.

"If you choose to believe in limits, you will live a limited life."

—Kevin Horsley
Unlimited Memory

There was no design to her life, and it came to me to ask her, **"When are you going to start living your life by design rather than happenstance?"** She exclaimed, "That's an 'ah-ha' moment!" That's what Tammy needed to hear to stop complaining and start designing a winning life.

However, this meant she had to make extremely difficult decisions in order to start living life by design. Living life by design means that you take the time to develop and create the important areas of your life. Living your life by design happens when you refuse to take the easy way. You refuse to just stand by and wait to see what life may or may not bring you.

Happenstance is when you live your life hoping to get lucky and meet the person of your dreams, to land your supreme job, career path, or entrepreneurial business of a lifetime. Typically, happenstance occurs without your awareness. So many of us have lived and can relate to the phenomenon of living by happenstance. It occurs when you allow things to happen to you without taking any agency over them.

Have you ever been fully invested in a close relationship only to have it crumble to the ground before your eyes? Have you wondered when and where the breakdown happened?

In the chapters that follow, Lisa and I will share intimate details from the breakdowns of some of our previous relationships. These are things we've all experienced, and they are some of the hardest things in life to face.

I sought out the help of the most highly recommended therapist that I could find. After a few sessions and hearing about the complex and difficult choice I had to make, my therapist asked me a question that I had never asked myself. She said, "What do you want?"

Wouldn't you think it would be easy to answer such a simple yet profound question? Even while attempting to provide a reasonable response, my answer was firmly seated in what I wanted for all involved except myself. She had to ask me the question three times before I could even hear the question, "What do YOU want?"

"Depression is the inability to construct a future."

—From the film
Side Effects,
(2013)

The clear help that was needed was at the foundational level of figuring out my own desires. It was daunting for me, and I wasn't able to continue therapy. These moments felt like a fast track to depression. In the world of psychology, I heard it said best, "Depression is the inability to construct a future." During this confusing time, my entire future was unclear. Was there a time in your life when you had no idea how to live into a healthy future or where to go to receive the right help?

I learned this resonating quote from the movie *Side Effects*. This is a 2013 American psychological thriller directed by Steven Soderbergh and written by

Scott Z. Burns. It stars Rooney Mara as a woman who is prescribed experimental drugs by psychiatrists. After watching some difficult and tragic scenes of her character battle depression, and although our lives didn't parallel, I was compelled to do my best to discover how to heal naturally.

I didn't believe that medications would solve my challenges and I did not want to get addicted to anything, so I had to start from scratch thinking about how to resolve this conflict. Somehow, someway, I had to figure out how to answer the simple question of what I wanted for myself.

I was a classic over-server, stricken with the disease to please and a perfectionist mentality. All of this was tied to playing my part very well in a dysfunctional, codependent relationship with my wife at the time. You may ask, what is the right thing to do? How do you manage such contradictions? How do you serve your highest wants and needs while seeking to remain respectful to all involved?

Matters like this aren't simple or easy, especially while deeply immersed in one of the worst recessions; my earnings were 30 percent of my normal earning potential. Closing down a twenty-five-year marriage while starting a brand-new beautiful relationship and seeking to maintain a healthy mental disposition feels like walking a tightrope staged at 10,000 feet in the air with no former training. In order to find my path through making the best and healthiest decisions for all, I chose to get on the path of becoming a recovering perfectionist and aspiring good-enoughist.

Thankfully, I learned this concept from the brilliance of Brené Brown and her inspiring book, *The Gifts of Imperfection*. Putting down my lifetime zeal of perfectionism was the best gift I had given others and myself at that point in my life. Perfectionism will drive you and everyone around you crazy!

I also chose to get in touch with my primary governing values and establish which roles I must start playing in my life and which dysfunctional roles I must eliminate. I weighed the quality of my governing values on a five-star rating system. Think of the five-star rating system like a five-star movie rating. Five stars represents the highest and best quality rating and one star represents the lowest quality. As you can imagine, the number of stars below five stars represent lower quality and value.

The next step was to weigh the quality of how I was performing in "walking the talk" of my values versus the roles that I was taking on or not taking on. There was a clear misalignment from my roles and values. In the absence of a qualified therapist, are you wondering how I discovered the perfect method of measuring my roles and values and looking for personal alignment between the two?

Knowing that I was finally on track to use a proven method to discover how to determine what I wanted, I had to do the work required to modify my behavior in order to create a positive alignment in my most important relationships. I knew I had to live into my highest roles and values.

Living your life by design starts with asking yourself a very important question: What do you want for and from your life? Understanding what you value most and the key roles you play in your life represents a solid foundation for personal fulfillment. This assessment means taking a close look at all of your roles and governing values. We learned this concept from Hyrum Smith in his book, *What Matters Most*.

After acquiring the What Matters Most philosophy from Hyrum Smith's book, I built a 5-Star What Matters Most Assessment to use as a tool to measure whether the roles that I was playing were in alignment with my value system. If you are seeking to establish alignment of your roles and value system along with an excellent foundation for personal fulfillment, follow the two-phase 5-Star What Matters Most Assessment steps below:

5-Star What Matters Most Assessment – Roles Phase I

1. List your most important roles
2. Using a 5-Star rating system, rate how important your roles are to you
3. Rate the performance of how well you are living into your roles
4. Write a brief description of why your roles are important to you
5. Group your roles based on similarity

5-Star What Matters Most Assessment – Values Phase II

1. List your most important values
2. Using a 5-Star rating system, rate how important your values are to you
3. Rate the performance of how well you are living into your values
4. Write a brief description of why your values are important to you
5. Group your values based on similarity

On the following page, please see an example of a completed 5-Star What Matters Most Assessment Phase I and II.

5-STAR WHAT MATTERS MOST ASSESSMENT—ROLES PHASE I

Count	Importance Level (0–5 stars)	Individual Roles	Performance Rating (0–5 stars)	Roles Sorted by Group
1	4.0	Chameleon	4.0	
2	4.0	Entertainer	3.8	
3	4.5	Humility	4.5	
4	5.0	Inspirer	4.0	Group 1 Character Role 8 Roles
5	4.5	Listener	4.5	
6	4.0	Peacemaker	4.2	
7	4.0	Role Model	4.5	
8	4.5	Transcending Race	4.0	
	4.3		**4.2**	
9	5.0	Educator	4.0	
10	5.0	Learner (Student)	4.0	Group 2 Educational Role 3 Roles
11	4.5	Reader	4.8	
	4.8		**4.3**	
12	4.0	Friend	4.5	
13	5.0	Husband	4.0	
14	5.0	Problem Solver	4.0	Group 3 Personal Relationships Role 5 Roles
15	4.0	Family Relative	4.0	
16	5.0	Relationship Manager	4.5	
	4.6		**4.2**	
17	4.0	Business Owner	4.0	
18	4.5	Coach	4.5	
19	4.5	Experienced Marketer	3.5	Group 4 Professional Role 5 Roles
20	4.0	Inspirational Leader & Speaker	4.0	
21	4.0	Partner	4.0	
	4.2		**4.0**	

Average Importance Level	Average Performance Rating
4.5	**4.2**

5-STAR WHAT MATTERS MOST ASSESSMENT—VALUES PHASE II

Count	Individual Governing Values	Value Rating	Governing Values Sorted by Priority & Group	Performance Rating	My Governing Values Statements & Why They Are Important To Me
1	Mental Health	5.0	**Health 3 Values**	4.0	Being mentally healthy allows me the proper mindset to work through or resolve all life matters in good spirit.
2	Physical Health	5.0		4.0	Maintaining good physical health gives me positive energy to live out a full range of unconstricting life choices.
3	Spiritual Health	5.0		4.5	Being spiritually connected allows me to accept, learn and live from unseen sources.
		5.0		**4.2**	
4	Faithfulness	5.0	**Authenticity 7 Values**	5.0	Faithfulness demonstrates your desire to be respectful and truthful to those you have agreements with.
5	Honesty	5.0		4.7	It allows others to build trust and offers communication and intention that they can count on.
6	Integrity	5.0		4.7	Integrity is couched in consistently doing what I have committed to do.
7	Peace of Mind	5.0		4.0	Good peace of mind allows me to live peacefully in my own skin.
8	Personal Responsibility	4.0		4.0	Personal responsibility is a measure of taking full ownership while remaining accountable.
9	Intuition	4.0		3.5	Tapping into intuition allows me to get in touch with my inner guiding system, using instincts and gut to guide me.
10	Time (the value & usage of time)	5.0		4.8	Time is the most precious commodity, it's perishable and invaluable. I honor, respect and use it wisely.
		4.7		**4.4**	
11	Equality	4.5	**Open Mindedness 3 Values**	5.0	Nobody is left out based on prejudice.
12	Level Playing Field	4.5		4.0	Everyone has a chance at winning.
13	Opportunity	5.0		4.0	The only shot at winning is by having opportunity to get in the game.
		4.7		**4.3**	

Count	Individual Governing Values	Value Rating	Governing Values Sorted by Priority & Group	Performance Rating	My Governing Values Statements & Why They Are Important To Me
14	Care	4.0		4.0	Care is important as it feeds a positive nature and investment in my relationships.
15	Compassion	4.0		4.0	Showing compassion adds value to my relationships allowing others to receive my support.
16	Generosity	4.0		4.7	Being generous leaves me feeling good to know that I'm helping others in their time of need or want.
17	Giving	4.0		4.7	Giving brings me great pleasure and demonstrates the depth of my care, it leaves me feeling good.
18	Love	5.0		4.5	Love is one of the deepest most positive emotions that touches us in a range of ways.
19	Purpose	5.0	Contribution 11 Values	5.0	Living into my purpose provides direction, creates meaning, and connects me to my vocation while serving self and others.
20	Self-preservation	5.0		5.0	Valuing self-preservation proves that we care and love ourselves enough to matter and continue striving for our best progression
21	Service	5.0		4.0	Good service is largely well received and most people value and appreciate it.
22	Sharing	4.0		3.5	Sharing allows a blissful exchange of important information and resources.
23	Supporting Key Relationships	4.0		4.0	Supporting key relationships brings pleasure on all sides.
24	The Power of Words	5.0		4.0	Respecting the power of words puts me in the driver seat to leave people and situations better than I found them.

Average Value Rating: **4.5**

Average Value Rating: 4.7

Average Performance Rating: **4.3**

Average Performance Rating: 4.3

If you want to download a free working version of our Five-Star What Matters Most Assessment, please go to www.jesstalk.com, click on the Resources tab, and then choose systems, tools, and processes.

Once you determine what you want for and from your life, the next step is to envision clearly what the final picture of what you want truly looks like. The steps following this perspective are to start building your life plan backward from your ultimate long-term vision of your life. We recommend including the following foundational basics in your life plan:

Why—Search inside yourself and determine your biggest why in your life plan. Ask and answer the question of why you want to pursue the lifestyle that you are choosing. Don't attempt to live into your best life by working through it all on your own. Start building your mastermind of people who you believe will support you and help you grow and develop and live into your best life plan now and into the future. Get on track with our development offering below.

BOST –
Background—Objective—Strategy—Tactics

Background—Start your plan by writing a description of the key personal and professional areas of growth and achievement that has allowed you to gain success up to your current place in life.

Objective—Write your clarifying objective that represents exactly what you plan to do in order to grow and continue developing to the next level.

Strategy—Create a written strategy for prioritizing key areas of your life to identify what is most important to you. For example, the following may represent key areas of your life that are important to you:

Family
Health
Professional Development
Relationships (intimate, friends, colleagues)
Education
Goals

You must establish how important each of the key areas of your life are as they are likely connected to one another. For example, you may push for professional development, but if you aren't respectful to saving time and space for managing your health and family, you may negatively impact these key areas and not maintain the proper connections. Managing these significant tie-backs to self and the people will help you as needed in meaningful areas of your life.

Tactics—Design clear, definable, and measurable processes to ensure the actions you take are in full alignment with your Objectives.

Strengths & Weaknesses—Ensure to include your strengths and weaknesses in order to know and share what you are good at and have a clear understanding of where you need to improve. If you aren't certain of what your strengths and weaknesses are, be willing to ask a few people that you have an excellent relationship with as they know you well. They may see things, talents, or areas of needed improvement that you can't see in yourself.

Goals—Consider the important goals you want to accomplish during your lifetime. Take another close look at your why, objective, strategy, values, and roles to help guide your creation and mapping out of your goals. You may want to write your goals down in different categories. Some examples of different goal categories may include the following:

Health—Ensure that you consult with a doctor or health professional on a regular basis.

Personal—Travel to Europe and visit Italy, France, Croatia, and Spain.

Spiritual—A feeling or belief that there is something greater than self that connects us all.

Physical—Being physically active, weight management, daily stretching, and workouts.

Professional—Strive for excellence in your field of study; increase your earnings.

Once you have written out your goals, the next step is to determine how you will accomplish your goals. Take an honest and clear assessment of where you stand right now. Use your life plan to help determine and write down what steps you are going to need to take in order to reach your goals and fully live into your life plan.

Creating your life plan is a predecessor to the roadmap of helping you to live your best life, offering the ability to adjust as needed. You will want to review your plan weekly and record your accomplishments and growth on a monthly basis. Remember that your life plan is a fluid process and ever changing.

A solid structure for building your life plan will include the following components:

1. 5-Year Outlook (long-term vision)
2. 3-Year Perspective (mid-term vision)
3. 1-Year View
4. 90-Day Plan (personal and professional)
5. Annual Book Reading List
6. Life Plan Benefits

On the following page, see an example of a completed life plan.

My 5-Year Outlook

Value	Goal	Why These Goals Are Important	What Kind of Person Must I Become to Reach Goal	Strategy
5	Change others' lives by my presence	Ability to help more people in a time efficient fashion	Must continue to be patient with others	Must always continue to be patient with others
4	Dramatically improve societies	To become a global presence	Must become and remain a learned and studied person	Gain connections with global leaders
4	Find a way to help make life complete for my parents	To repay the gift of life	Become more available and increase my exposure to both of them	Start by blocking weekend visits now
4	Set many new paradigms in creative thinking	To help bring about positive change	I must remain clear and focused, surrounded by other positive lights	Block time for silence and thinking moments daily, starting today
4.5	Become financially independent	To serve self and others at the highest levels	Open for growth and learning financial intelligence. Connect with the best financial advisors	Leave our routine financial advisor and hire new intelligent advisor who cares about us

4.3   **Average Value Rating**

Value	Value Legend
5	**Highest Value and Impact**
4	**High Value and Impact**
3	**Important Value and Impact**
2	**Modestly Valuable**
I	**Significant**

My 3-Year Perspective

Value	Goal	Why These Goals Are Important	What Kind of Person Must I Become to Reach Goal	Strategy
5	Become a person of great influence	Allowing others to help make my life better and use my best talents to improve their lives	Ask higher powers for the direction and path to follow	Start looking for powerful people to welcome into my village
5	Become well spoken, educated, healthy, strong, energetic	This helps to demonstrate the making of a legend	Someone who shares the best modeling concepts	Find the best role models and examples of excellent character today
5	Redefine Leadership	There is no reason we have to keep the same archetypes	I must learn from the masters while creating a new model	Attend the best leadership conferences and read the best leadership books daily
4	Pay back our clients 100-fold	Pay it forward program	Remain open to support all people and discover the best resources to share and serve others	Never forget the power of my global village
4	Learn to write effectively and passionately	Writing effectively and passionately allows me to communicate effectively and reach a broad range of audiences	I must write from the heart	Write a minimum of one hour per day, every day

4.6   **Average Value Rating**

Value	Value Legend
5	**Highest Value and Impact**
4	**High Value and Impact**
3	**Important Value and Impact**
2	**Modestly Valuable**
1	**Significant**

My 1-Year View

Value	Goal	Why These Goals Are Important	What Kind of Person Must I Become to Reach Goal	Strategy
5	We maintain a healthy body, mind, and spirit	To create a biobalanced state of being	One who seeks continual improvement	We share health meetings every Sunday
5	We resonate at positive energy levels	This energy is therapeutic to all others, even with no direct conversation with them	This supports us seeking to help many people	Check in with our accountability partners regarding how our energy resonates
4	We consistently lead leaders	To assure our talents and abilities are appreciated and stimulated	Strong, consistent, clear, and concise communicators	We practice strengthening our communication muscles daily
4	We help our family live their best lives now	To assist them with living happy lives	Ready to help whenever they are ready to grow and learn	Remain open for the opportunity to serve others
4	We write creatively, affectionately, effectively, and passionately	To reach other audiences who may be helped by our writings	Continue the practice of writing and securing help to improve	Maintain this as a daily practice

4.4   Average Value Rating

Value	Value Legend
5	Highest Value and Impact
4	High Value and Impact
3	Important Value and Impact
2	Modestly Valuable
1	Significant

MY LIFE PLAN EXAMPLE

Areas	90-Day Plan
Area #1	**Health & Wellness Plan**
1	I am meditating for 21 days for the Oprah—Deepak Chopra relationship challenge.
2	I am reading to understand and know all 7 Chakras how they work.
3	I am working out and getting the proper daily rest to insure optimum health, wellness, favor, grace, and peace.
4	I am attending yoga one to two times per week schedule it with Christy.
5	I am scheduling a family dinner once a month.
6	I am continuing to eat 3 healthy meals 6 days per week in order to achieve and maintain my goal weight of 125 lbs. in 8 months.
7	I am educating myself by reading Dr. Jon Barron's book recommended by Paul Grady.
8	I am reading one hour per day in order to get into Ayurvedic alignment, as well as living the lifestyle for my type of food to eat.
Area #2	**Personal & Professional Development Plan**
1	I surround myself with top executives and like-minded individuals (the information exchange develops my full self).
2	I invest two hours per day in business development (coaching, networking, and structural redevelopment) 5 days per week
3	I am building Conversations into a paid platform and new product development through JessTalk & LisaListen.
4	I am committed to the What Matter Most program and submitting to 3 success coaching sessions per month.
5	I am mastering my elevator speech and will have it fully developed and memorized by the end of the month.
6	I am networking and researching with coaches at least twice per month in order to continue to develop my business and coaching style.
7	I am committed to writing in my journal 15 minutes 4 days per week.
8	I am developing my life vision for health, professional life, finances, travel.
Area #3	**Financial Development Plan**
1	My goal of reaching financial independence is supported by my financial freedom objectives and I review them with my partner daily.
2	I am continuing my path to financial intelligence, budgeting, reading, and paying attention to the law and energy of money.
3	I am reviewing our Cash Flow Statement monthly with Robert Lee & Associates Accounting Firm.
4	I am disciplined to collaborate with and review our Cash Flow Statement with my partner weekly.
5	I am reading a minimum of 1 financial intelligence book per month.
6	My credit card balances are kept to a zero balance and paid weekly.
7	I have made a commitment to pay myself first (20% of my gross earnings) every month.
8	I maintain positive growth in my bank accounts.
9	I am focused on building multiple streams of additional income.

My Life Plan Benefits

1	Master Organizational System—Designed for achieving life goals and development
2	Shifting Priorities—Rank and priority system allowing you to manage a world of shifting priorities
3	Creative Thinking—Dedicated use of this life plan adds a major assist in clearing your mind and adds accountability
4	Set The Table—My life plan is constantly showing me personal and professional growth
5	Targets and deadlines—My life plan helps me stay focused on my targets and deadlines

Book Reading Recommendations

	Recommended Books	Author
1	*15 Invaluable Laws of Growth*	John Maxwell
2	*A Complaint Free World*	Will Bowen
3	*Action Strategies For Personal Achievement*	Brian Tracy
4	*Authenticity*	Ron Willingham
5	*Born A Crime*	Trevor Noah
6	*Change Your Thinking Change Your Life*	Brian Tracy
7	*Chop Wood Carry Water*	Joshua Medcalf
8	*Fair Play*	Eve Rodsky
9	*Giftology*	John Ruhlin
10	*How Successful People Think*	John C. Maxwell
11	*Leader Shift*	John Maxwell
12	*Measure What Matters*	John Doerr
13	*Mindsight*	Daniel J. Siegel, M.D.
14	*Napoleon Hill's Golden Rules*	Napoleon Hill
15	*Solve For Happy*	Mo Gawdat
16	*The Fifth Agreement*	Don Miguel Ruiz & Don Jose Ruiz
17	*The Four Agreements*	Don Miguel Ruiz
18	*The Grief Recovery Handbook*	John W. James, Russell Friedman
19	*The Power of Full Engagement*	Jim Loehr & Tony Schwartz
20	*Unlimited Memory*	Kevin Horsley
21	*What Matters Most*	Hyrum Smith

The reality is that you will likely incur failures and set-backs as you live into your life plan. Don't allow break-downs and setbacks to derail you from your life plan. See any failure as a learning opportunity and determine where, when, and how to enroll your new lessons into your adjusted life plan.

Then start living your plan from where you are, mak-ing the necessary changes as life circumstances dictate based on your ultimate vision for getting what you want for and from your life.

From the countless clients we have served in our pro-fessional coaching business, those clients that achieved the highest level of living into the life they designed chose accountability partners to help encourage and champion their development.

The best way to improve the odds of living your life by design is to add the special resource of an accountability partner whom you love and trust. Launch an agreement with your accountability partner that their number one role is to hold your feet to the fire and not let you off the hook regarding staying the course throughout your entire plan.

You are likely running your life through the false limit-ing beliefs that you may have been taught early in life. One example of a false limiting belief would be the idea that in order to get a good job and make a lot of money, you have to get good grades in high school so that you can go to college. We call this predominantly taught standard of life the old GRASP concept. GRASP stands for Getting Ready, Attitude, Signature, and Passion.

It isn't common for people to place a name on the con-cept of being taught these false limiting beliefs. We have seen a major universal connection to this concept that is consistently being taught. As mentioned above, we call this the old GRASP. In the aforementioned example, we are chiefly focused on getting good grades in school and working many years after getting a good job with no plans for the future beyond the good grades and good job.

Our attitudes are focused on a tired and worn-out form of the ideal life. In mindsets like this, we don't focus on building our personal brand, what we call our signature. Without the consistent adjustment of an attractive and positive attitude supported by the knowledge of our unique signature, we have no passion for life beyond the old GRASP life concept.

By adopting the new form of GRASP, you move beyond the common life roadmap and focus beyond getting good grades during your early Getting Ready stages of life. You become intentional about upgrading your attitude and discovering your signature in order to have an opportunity to continue improving your signature and live into your life with passion.

We are not submitting scientific evidence that retiring and doing nothing equates to death. Over our fifty-five years of serving and witnessing countless lives, we have seen those following the old GRASP concept die within six years of retiring. We believe that following the old GRASP model puts you in the front seat for living a life of happenstance. In this context as previously noted, happenstance means that you go along in life just waiting to see what happens, what comes your way in terms of jobs, careers, relationships, and other life matters.

In order to avoid the trap, we recommend that you adopt and adapt to the new form of GRASP. The new form of GRASP is simply choosing to live your life by design!

It starts with a reinvigorated form of Getting Ready, by using a fresh set of eyes to look at the A in the center of GRASP. As noted, this A stands for Attitude. In the new concept of GRASP, we ask you to take a close look at your current attitude about important life matters.

If you are in a bad place, choose to take a close look at what is causing you to be in such a bad place. Once you discover what this is, pick a qualified accountability partner, life coach, or counselor to help you make the necessary corrective steps to improve. If you are in a good space following your self-review of your attitude, make the choice to move from good to great and follow the same process to develop and grow as noted previously.

After ensuring that you have effectively leveled up your attitude, it's time to look at your signature. Your signature is made up of the things that make you uniquely you. It is exclusive to you and showcases how people come to know you. The following is represented in your signature:

Character
Best gifts and talents
How you show up with others
Your personal brand
How you leave others feeling
Your communication style
Your distinctive identification of who you are as a person

Your main objective is to continue developing your signature to the degree that you always leave people wanting more...wanting more of you and your presence in their lives.

The P portion of our GRASP concept is Passion. As you embark on the path of discovering and developing your Passion, it will add value to all other segments of GRASP. As you apply your Passion across the path of Getting Ready, Attitude, and Signature, you become more engaging and positively infectious.

Identifying what ignites your Passion can also be the path to tapping into your best gifts and talents, which can direct you to living into your purpose. We are all blessed with some type of talent, something that we do better than most, if not all others. As you connect Passion to purpose, you become inspired to live an awesome life and accomplish greatness! Choosing to dial into the new GRASP concept can change your definition of how to live a happy life that far exceeds simply making money for a living.

So many of us have been lulled into believing that making a lot of money is the answer to a happy life. I discovered a passage in a great documentary featuring a world-class boxer, Hector Macho Camacho. When speaking about Hector's triumphant and tragic life, his closest friend, Rudy Gonzalez, said, "You could have everything in the world and still have nothing and money does not make you happy, it only buys you time to realize that you aren't happy. When there is a thing that lives inside of you, it doesn't leave!" That thing that Rudy Gonzalez was speaking of was the unmanaged inner demons that can haunt you for life if not reconciled or dealt with.

Hector Macho Camacho was killed at the age of fifty in Puerto Rico, and even though he made millions of dollars as a nearly unbeatable fighter, he was never able to get in touch with his inner feelings and manage them to live a happy life by design. He didn't allow his amazing athletic talent to pave a life of happiness. Unfortunately, he suffered from drug addiction, which prevented him from enjoying a beautiful life he started to build with his wife and children.

"You could have everything in the world and still have nothing and money does not make you happy, it only buys you time to realize that you aren't happy. When there is a thing that lives inside of you, it doesn't leave!"

—Rudy Gonzalez

"*In order to start living your life by design, you will want to check into what is going on in your Head, Heart, and Gut (HHG).*"

—Lisa Ferrell

Lisa says it best: "In order to start living your life by design, you will want to check into what is going on in your Head, Heart, and Gut (HHG)." This is a concept that we use to check in with our mental thoughts and emotional feelings, along with our instinct and intuition. You will make consistent great life choices by using the daily practice of tuning into the HHG concept. Then, as explained above, you weigh the quality of how you are performing in walking the talk of your values versus the roles that you are taking on or not taking on.

While you likely know how to check into what is going on in your head and heart, you may not realize the full value of checking into what is going on inside your gut. We will discuss the connection of how your gut can serve like a second brain in the following chapter.

Summary Points

Living Life by Design

1. Living life by design means that you take the time to develop and create the important areas of your life. Happenstance is when you live your life just taking what life throws your way. Typically, happenstance occurs without your awareness.

2. "Depression is the inability to construct a future." During the most difficult times of life, if you don't have the ability to visualize or build a future, you are likely battling depression and professional help is greatly needed. If you are not depressed but confused about how to begin to design your life, use our five-star value rating system to align your deepest beliefs to your behavior.

3. Head, Heart, and Gut (HHG) is the path to understanding yourself and what truly motivates you. This is a concept that we use to check in with our thoughts and emotions along with instinct and intuition.

Key Action Steps

Living Life by Design

1. Take a close look at how you are living your life and ask yourself, "What do you want?"

2. Compare the roles you are playing in life to your strongest values. Are they counter to one another?

3. Learn to trust your instincts, and move toward aligning your behavior and decisions with them. Fully embrace the new GRASP concept and use it in your life!

Chapter 2

Trusting Your Gut Instincts

I recently discovered some interesting research from the Cleveland Clinic,[1] noting that our gut serves much like having a second brain. Have you ever experienced the power of intuition in your gut where you just knew something without previously experiencing it? The brain interprets gut signals as emotions. Learning to trust your gut is best when making important life choices.

Have you experienced butterflies in your stomach over a matter or occurrence that was telling you something powerful? It's like those times when you have gone with a decision about something based on a compelling feeling in your gut shaping your choice. Have you ever wondered why that was? Hidden in the walls of your digestive system are the links between digestion, mood, health, and the way you think. Scientists call the small brain that you feel in your gut the Enteric Nervous System (ENS). It is a powerful brain connection system.

The ENS is made up of two thin layers of more than one-hundred million nerve cells. These nerve cells are lining your gastrointestinal tract running from your esophagus to rectum.[2] Science is starting to understand the brain/gut connection and how it affects our behavior, responses, reactions, temperament, and moods. It is also referred to as the brain and gut connection. The nutrients that we consume are absorbed through our intestines and fuel our brains.

Our brains take up a very small portion of our total body weight and take up approximately 20 percent of the energy we take in.[3] Nutrients make a major difference in the way our brains function on a daily basis.[4]

As we are growing in the womb, the ENS and the Central Nervous System (CNS) develop from the same tissue. In many respects, its structure mirrors that of the brain in that it has sensory and motor neurons supported by a protective structure of glial cells, which acts a bit like scaffolding. These two systems mirror one another. The ENS uses many of the same neurotransmitters to function, such as serotonin and dopamine.

Did you know that there is an information superhighway from your gut to your brain? I trust you will make this connection and make great use of the connection between your gut and brain choices on this biological superhighway! The simplest way to complete positive action and important life choices when it comes to the connection from your gut and brain is to respect your intuition. It typically feels like your intuition is present in your gut during those times when you have a feeling about a matter without necessarily having the understanding of knowing why or how you have the feeling and associated knowledge.

I have often used my intuition to make important life decisions, and I can't recall a time when I trusted and acted upon my intuition and the relating matter failed as a result of my choice of actions. I can, however, recall countless times when I had an intuition and either ignored it or chose to make choices counter to the inner knowledge couched in my intuition. The moral of this story, learn to trust and act on the brain and gut connection otherwise known as the power of your intuition.

Speaking of making important life choices, we would be remiss if we didn't mention the commanding effect of serotonin in our brains and decision-making process. Serotonin is the key hormone that stabilizes our mood, feelings of well-being, and happiness. This hormone impacts our entire body. It enables brain cells and other nervous system cells to communicate with each other. Serotonin also helps with sleeping, eating, and digestion.[5]

It's important to know that 95 percent of your body's serotonin can be found in the gut.[6] Serotonin is that marvelous mood molecule affected by antidepressant drugs (selective serotonin reuptake inhibitors [SSRIs] such as Prozac). SSRIs block the reabsorption (reuptake) of serotonin into neurons. This makes more serotonin available to improve transmission of messages between neurons. SSRIs are called selective because they mainly affect serotonin, not other neurotransmitters.[7] It's no wonder that diet, medications, and antibiotics can wreak havoc on one's mood. There is a clear connection with serotonin and dopamine.

Serotonin is the anti-impulse agent, the soother, the quieter. It darkens the landscape. We need it when we are overwhelmed by too much at once and our thoughts become obsessive or overloaded. Serotonin constrains dopamine's actions, decreases our focus, and limits our ability to make connections with other parts of the brain. Too little serotonin makes us irritable, our annoyance threshold goes down, and we can be drawn into action in an instant. A low level of serotonin allows for so many connections to be made that too much becomes significant! Our thoughts either become obsessive, or our brain becomes overloaded and cannot process anything.

With the understanding of how in sync our heads and guts are, I launched an effort to swiftly start living my life by design based on the truth of where I stood with personal alignment. This intentional self-study led me to choose divorce in what was clearly a failed and non-repairable relationship.

After checking into all three key areas of HHG, I chose to connect with my intuition and work on what matters most with the main objective of securing alignment between my roles and governing values.

Summary Points

Trusting Your Gut Instincts

1. Along with head and heart, science is starting to understand the brain-gut access and how it affects our behavior, responses, reactions, temperament, and moods. It is also referred to as the brain and gut connection.

2. Serotonin has a commanding effect in our brains and decision-making process. Serotonin is the key hormone that stabilizes our mood, feelings of well-being, and happiness. This hormone impacts the entire body. It enables brain cells and other nervous system cells to communicate with each other. Serotonin also helps with sleeping, eating, and digestion.

3. Knowing and understanding that these elements and others create an information superhighway from your gut to your brain is key in helping you start trusting your gut instincts. Learning to value and use this information about your gut and brain choices puts you in the driver's seat on this biological superhighway!

Key Action Steps

Trusting Your Gut Instincts

1. Notice when you feel the brain-gut connection, such as when a tightness in your stomach

or chest occurs when something undesirable is about to happen.

2. Research what maintaining a healthy diet looks like for you, since the nutrients we consume are absorbed through our intestines and fuel our brains.

3. Include your gut feelings and intuition in the Head, Heart, and Gut (HHG) intentional self-study to discover more about your personal values and "what you truly want."

Chapter 3

Building Relationship Equity

Relationship equity is similar to the equity a home-owner builds up when they make upgrades and investments in their home. I am fortunate to have a shining example of relationship equity in my relationship with my life partner. Lisa provides a lifetime of opportunity with which to build and maintain infectious relationship equity. She is a trusted universal partner, and I'm very fortunate for her solid presence in my life. We trust that you will want to bring relationship equity to your personal and professional connections.

Over time, you add on assets to your home. You may build an outdoor patio in your backyard. You may consider adding a three-car garage or an indoor gym. Each improvement that you make adds to the equity and the market value of your home, just as quality investments made in your associations with others raises the significance of the relationship while increasing value on all sides.

Every interaction and decision related to your relationships is an opportunity to build value through understanding, trust, and respect. As you witness and internalize the power of relationship equity, infuse this same construction effort in all of your affiliations. Thus, providing value, growth, warmth, longevity, and excitement toward the development of and for your relationships.

The reason that building relationship equity matters is based on the simple fact that you can't continue to drain the emotional bank accounts without ever making deposits or investments into those important relationships. Without deposits, you will eventually become overdrawn, and you could potentially lose key relationships.

One of Lisa's longtime friendships comes to mind when I think about relationship equity. Lisa will share how she has built relationship equity with her lifetime friend, Ida.

"Ida championed my cause in 1979. She got me a job interview at the local TV station where she worked. Who knew this interview would land me a 35-year career in broadcasting?

I started as a traffic coordinator. I was so excited to land this job. I logged all of the commercials that came into the station. I was later promoted to a sales assistant and stayed with the station for four years. Ida is still with this television station today.

Ida and I would go to lunch together and hang out on weekends with our significant others. We went on many boating trips in Lake Powell and had weekend sleepovers. We were all very tight. I asked her to go to lunch with me one day. I said I was going to Planned Parenthood for a pregnancy test, and she said, 'What? I think I'm pregnant too!'

We both got pregnancy tests and found out that day that we were both pregnant. Neither of us had planned this at all. It was fun to share this special time in life. We understood each other with almost no words spoken. I had my daughter, Porsha, one week before she had her daughter, Dante. Our daughters have grown up together and are very close and share the relationship equity concept.

Ida and I have had our ups and downs in our friendship over the last forty-two years. There were times that we went years without talking to one another. It wasn't because of anything that happened between us, but because my ex-husband and Ida's husband had a falling out, which naturally affected us. Through it all, our friendship has stood the test of time.

We picked up right where we left off whenever we would get together. It was as if no time had passed. I can't tell you how many times I've moved in my life, and Ted and Ida have been there for 80 percent of these moves. Most recently, my mother moved from Salt Lake City to Las Vegas, and Ida was right there by our sides, packing and moving boxes into the pod.

After we packed up mom's belongings, Jesse, mom, and I went to stay at Ida's gorgeous new home. She fixed us a fantastic array of fresh vegetables out of her garden and fresh salmon Ted caught in Alaska. After dinner, we sat on her deck and enjoyed the fresh mountain air. We shared stories of our past and had many belly laughs over a nice glass of wine.

Ida and I were both excellent about giving and taking in our friendship. It was never lopsided and had a flow and rhythm to it. It feels effortless. We both subscribe to building relationship equity within our friendship without keeping score. We both give to one another because we want to add continual value to each other's lives."

Can you think of a friendship you have where you share such a synergy and flow? If you answer yes, know that you have likely built outstanding relationship equity within those friendships. If you can't think of a friendship like that, then it's time for you to start building relationship equity in your most important connections. A path for getting started is through ICE.

ICE – 3 Principles of Creating Relationship Equity

In our effort to help you to take a deep dive in understanding how you may **ICE** your most important relationship with self and others, consider the following:

I – Investing in Self and Others

Depending on the nature of your personality and life circumstances, investing in yourself may fall near the end of your list, or you may not even place yourself on your list.

Whenever Lisa and I are given the opportunity to serve a personal or professional development coaching client and we ask them to name their top three priorities, 99 percent of the time they never include themselves in their list of top priorities.

Are you part of that 99 percent? If you answered yes, our ICE principle is worth your consideration. If you have answered no to this question, then congratulations, you fall into the rare one percent of people who prioritize themselves in a healthy manner.

Many times, people will list God, children, parents, or jobs. The question I ask you to consider now is: how much more value could you give to your chosen faith, parents, children, businesses, or jobs if you consistently took care of yourself first? What are your top three life priorities? Take a few minutes to consider the question before continuing.

Lisa and I have both earned scholarly master's degrees in the unhealthy science of "disease to please" while obsessively seeking to satisfy others. It took us countless years to curtail our "disease to please" internal mechanism. We never considered asking ourselves what it would take to make our own lives a top-level priority.

Here's another universal truth: you likely won't get what you don't ask for! You've got to be willing to ask for what you want and need...consistently! Building relationship equity for yourself is just as important as building it with others.

In order to seek the best life balance and quest for investing in self and others, start putting yourself first by using the concept of extreme self-care in order to better serve yourself and others. In order to see examples of self-care, refer back to our self-care recommendations at the beginning of this chapter.

You will see and feel a profound internal turnaround and have a healthier disposition while serving yourself and others. It's like having unlimited emotional bank accounts.

You will not likely bounce checks when withdrawing from your well-funded emotional accounts. The best and most successful business professionals choose to pay themselves first. We recommend that you consider adopting this same philosophy.

Whether you are single, married with or without children, and regardless of the size of your personal or professional commitments—choose to pay yourself first. Start with allotting a minimum amount of time for yourself on a daily basis. Make this commitment to yourself nonnegotiable.

Find a way to ensure that your significant others know your plan to dedicate a percentage of each day to yourself. It will be life-changing to put this one action into motion. It works best to start with a reasonable allotment of time. Your inner resources will grow when you choose to dedicate your energy toward yourself. Lisa and I currently live by the 2–4 Self-Time concept. We are dedicated to spending two to four hours of time on ourselves on a daily basis.

What is the point of working smart and hard for forty to sixty hours a week if you are in a senior manager, entrepreneur, or business owner role? The point is to have an occupation allowing you to live a joyful and healthy life! Many of us miss this key point of why we seek an occupation and remain stuck in the daily grind. We often forget to block time on our calendar to simply do what we want and need to do.

Whenever you take time to decompress and nurture yourself, your resiliency will return. During these times, you may meditate, create a no-talking zone, read, listen to soft music, do absolutely nothing, create, visit with a best friend that you rarely get to connect with, journal your thoughts, or simply just remain quiet.

The Self-Time concept works best by choosing to start with a minimum of thirty minutes per day and gradually adding more time. When we blocked out our first thirty minutes of Self-Time, it seemed like an eternity. We are now up to two to four hours of Self-Time daily, and it feels like the blink of an eye! Use your own intuition as to how much time you would like to dedicate for your Self-Time.

You simply bring a better you back to all of your personal or professional commitments when you become consistent with practicing the lost art of the Self-Time.

One strategy for learning how to set aside time for yourself is to "Learn what's fueling you." This is a concept developed by Cheryl Richardson, a *New York Times* best-selling author who wrote *Take Time for Your Life*. Cheryl's inspiring book focuses on a seven-step program to help you create the life you want. If you are struggling with setting aside time for yourself, Cheryl's book is a must read!

C – Care About Self and Others

Choosing to care about self and others is a magical connection to our How You Leave Them Feeling concept.

As mentioned in the introduction, it's truly about how you leave yourself and others feeling that will allow you to build the best relationship equity with self and others. As basic as the principle of caring is, you may be surprised by the number of people who don't know how to care for themselves or others. Two key ingredients to showing how much you care are developing an active listening ear and asking intuitive questions.

It's also about keeping it simple! The caring portion of our **ICE** principal is couched in using the care principal much like the law of parsimony or the simplicity principle, which is also called Ockham's Razor.[8] Scholastic philosopher William of Ockham is credited with founding the law of parsimony, which states the idea that simpler explanations of observations should be preferred to more complex ones.

After more than thirty years of working with others in developing their personal and professional growth, we find many people tend to overcomplicate things. Rather than allowing yourself to fall into this majority, choose to simplify matters as often as possible.

Another description of Ockham's Razor says the best explanation is the one that requires you to make the fewest possible assumptions about what's involved. In order to keep us on pace for living our best life now, we remain respectful and intentional about practicing and continually getting better about how we leave ourselves and others feeling.

E – Extreme Self-Care

We are asking that you strongly consider making time to take extreme care of yourself as you continue the path of building very healthy relationships in the quest to enrich your life and others. Keep it simple and mirror the law of parsimony: You must care about yourself and others in order to live a joyful and enriched life!

We are naturally designed for survival, and taking care of ourselves is something that comes as part of the code written into the history of our biology. Some people may label this as being selfish, self-centered, or narcissistic. These are negative labels that don't bring positive favor within relationships. However, we believe the central root of this behavior has a healthy beginning; it is couched in taking care of our survival needs.

Getting our basic human needs met ensures that our species survives. These needs take the form of sex for procreation, obtaining food and water, and discovering a way to make a living in order to obtain shelter. In essence, getting our foundational needs met covers the basics of practical self-care and ensures that you care enough to sustain an essential level of life.

We believe practicing self-care and educating others on how to practice self-care has absolutely nothing to do with undesirable behaviors such as being selfish, self-centered, or narcissistic. Self-care is defined exactly as it is written: the practice of taking care of yourself.

We call it **extreme self-care** because you can never wear it out, and it is the root ingredient to choosing to deliver great relationship equity with self and others. It is a major universal life principle based on developing a resilient strategy to stand the test of time, regardless of life-challenging matters that may befall you.

The reality is that the longer you live, the more of life circumstances and experiences you will face. You will encounter losses, wins, fears, the end of important rela-tionships, extraordinary positive events, health scares, accidents, and more.

All of what was previously mentioned is part of the life that many of us know and live. So many people get lost and stuck in living into what has happened to them or what is happening to them, rather than shifting their focus to living their lives by design! From the countless people who we have served over the years, we see others remaining stuck in 10 percent of what may be causing disruptions in their life, versus putting 90 percent of their effort into what they can do about it.

Most people spend the majority of their time and effort being stuck like deer in the headlights while unknowingly stuck in the 10 percent of their life that is negative. While this phenomenon is unfortunately amped up, your life takes a swift positive shift whenever you choose to move over to the 90 percent side of this equation and start living your life focused on what you will do about what has happened or what is happening to you.

Developing resiliency requires you to stand up to and get beyond the opposing forces that have the potential to drive you into a negative funk. The practice of extreme self-care is the road map to your personal best health-connecting resiliency. Self-care has the three principles that create relationship equity within yourself and with others.

When you choose to add any or all of the self-care recommendations below to your daily routine, you will experience a more vibrant energy within yourself. If you don't choose self-care, it may be easy for you to fall into unhealthy patterns such as being insecure, unaware, self-consciousness, or anxious.

Practicing self-care involves the following:

1. Developing emotional intelligence (EI). Healthy EI offers you the ability to understand and manage your own emotions in positive ways

while communicating effectively with others to defuse conflict.

2. Learning to be compassionate with yourself.
3. Practicing good sleeping habits and taking respectful breaks throughout your day.
4. Making gut checks and being mindful of adopting healthy eating choices.
5. Cutting out negative self-talk by discovering your best assets and living from what you do have, not from what you don't have.
6. Reserving self-time. Block time on your calendar just for yourself and use this time to do only what you want to do to serve yourself.
7. Adding meditation to your daily routine, even if you choose only fifteen to thirty minutes per day, will be rejuvenating.
8. Nurturing your basic physical needs by walking, biking, or other daily exercises to maintain good physical health.
9. Considering your psychological development. Take part in activities to grow your mental state such as movies, plays, books, and special events.
10. Cultivating resiliency. Continue discovering ways to become more resilient by not allowing life difficulties to bring you to your knees.

Practicing our ICE principles can reduce your problem-solving stress levels. We have felt and hear from others that whenever you solve one problem, another two problems turn up for you to solve. This is an endless cycle repeated throughout our lives, and it is never ending. The better you get at solving problems in a simple rather than complicated fashion, the better your life will become.

It would be best if you made consistent investments in yourself and others while fueling your relationships with genuine and authentic caring for yourself and others.

President Theodore Roosevelt said, "People don't care how much you know until they know how much you care." Much like the Lisa and Ida story, you want to leave people feeling like you know them, understand them, and get them. So many of us wish to be understood.

Lisa and I have built amazing relationship equity in our own marriage by faithfully and diligently trying to understand one another and truly getting to know one another. We consistently practice the SHAVE concept. Five additional key traits to building relationship equity are Sincere, Humble, Authentic, Vulnerable and Engaging (SHAVE). When you bring these traits to your relationships, you will find more meaningful connections with others and the ability to sustain those connections.

Consider giving a sincere compliment to the people you are meeting. You may say something like, "Your hair looks great," "You have an amazing smile," or "I love your shoes." Seek to find a common denominator, and your conversations will take off naturally.

Enrolling this concept with complete authenticity is a great icebreaker and leaves others feeling great about themselves and good about you. You will leave them feeling warm and cozy right from the start. Also, consider meeting in a pleasant physical environment, setting the ambiance right from the start.

The following is an excellent illustration from Lisa regarding how she always practices building great relationships.

"From my sales days, whenever I saw a prospective client, I always bought from them first. This is how I would establish a relationship with them by being their customer first and frequenting their store. This would

"People don't care how much you know until they know how much you care."

—President Theodore Roosevelt

let them know that I invested and believed in their product.

I would get to know their staff, and I always had the rule of going three-deep in a company. First and foremost, get to know the gatekeeper, the owner, and the manager. The gatekeeper knows the ins and outs of what goes on. When you win this person over, then you have the opportunity for them to share the best time to get in touch with the decision maker and get an appointment.

After nurturing the relationship and feeling comfortable, I would then ask them questions about things I knew were important to them. It could be their children or their favorite sports team; you can just look around their office to see clues to things that are of interest to them and ask relevant questions. You can see if they have a degree on the wall or a picture of their children or grandchildren. People always love to talk about themselves. The most important advice I can give you is to be a good listener. If you listen well and long enough, you will build trust and likability.

No one likes to have someone come in and talk non-stop. It is imperative to create a great volley in your conversations. The most important word in everyone's vocabulary is his or her first name. Whenever you can refer to your client, friend, neighbor etc. with their first name, it leaves a lasting impression.

The other aspect of talking with this person is to know their character and learn what makes them tick. In other words, try to understand why they do what they do, understanding their DCM (Driving Core Motive). You will learn more about DCM in Chapter 6, entitled Color Code Personality Assessment.

We chose to become certified Color Code Trainers in order to ensure that we continued to learn and use this amazing system, tool, and process at the highest levels of all of our relationships. It allows us to quickly learn to speak the language of others. We continue to work on raising our ability to know exactly which language to speak with others in personal and professional endeavors."

Summary Points

Building Relationship Equity

1. Building relationship equity with a friend or partner is similar to building up financial equity in your home except it refers to people. As you add on, the value increases. Every interaction and every decision made related to that relationship is an opportunity to build understanding, trust, and respect.

2. Use the ICE principles to assist in building relationship equity. They include "Investing in yourself and others," "Caring about yourself and others," and "Extreme self-care." Only through true caring for your own welfare and those around you can you develop the qualities needed for healthy relationships.

3. SHAVE is five key traits to building relationship equity. They are being Sincere, Humble, Authentic, Vulnerable, and Engaging. When you bring these traits to your relationships, you will find more meaningful connections with others and the ability to sustain those connections.

Key Action Steps

Building Relationship Equity

1. This is an excellent time to pause your reading and ask yourself which of your important relationships you should take a close look at and make the needed changes, upgrades, or transformations.

2. Follow the advice of Ockham's Razor and try to keep your relationships with others as simple as possible. Be honest, straightforward, kind, and make an effort to understand others' points of view.

3. Take time for yourself. Self-Time works best by starting with a minimum of thirty minutes per day completely devoted to what you want to do. Gradually add more time to this commitment so you can serve your highest wants and needs.

Chapter 4

The Umuntu Factor

You may have experienced at times in your life what feels like an electrical connection with another person, maybe a complete stranger. You may feel inexplicably drawn to them, like you have some invisible bond. This happened to Lisa at a retreat we attended hosted by author and relationship consultant Barbara De Angelis in San Diego, California.

Lisa explains, "Barbara asked us to walk around and find one person to connect with. She guided us to look into that person's eyes while holding both of their hands. She continued to say, 'no matter what you do, do not let go and do not stop looking into each other's eyes.'

Barbara asked us to walk around and find one person to connect with.

I was enchantingly guided to this beautiful soul, and I felt pulled toward her. This remarkable soul goes by the name of Penny. We were totally drawn to one another in perfect alignment and agreement. This happened without any thought or words.

As we stared into each other's eyes, our connection was being fueled by new heartwarming energy that changed our body chemistry. Next came the tears which started streaming from her eyes with sympathetic resonance. A stream of endless tears came from my eyes as well.

The heat we were both generating between us was electrifying. It got so hot that we wanted to let go, but we stayed the course and kept holding on. The heat radiating from both of us became nearly unbearable to the point of being very uncomfortable.

When we were told to let go, we let go and immediately embraced each other. We held this heart-to-heart connection for what seemed like hours, but it was only for several minutes. It was an exceptional, energetic, and magical mutual exchange. This was a new expression that neither of us had ever experienced before.

Later that day, Penny joined us for lunch. She thanked me for the amazing connection and said that exchange unlocked something inside her that she had been struggling with for years.

Shadowing this experience during a lunch connection with five other retreat participants (including Jesse), Penny's energy continued to resonate. It was as though she was under a supernatural influence, offering a glorious inner shining of her soul and body from head to toe."

The value of that experience was instrumental in Lisa's argument to convince me to join Penny for an amazing adventure in South Africa. I was initially resistant to the idea based on the high cost and the unfortunate financial challenges that we were faced with at the time. I changed my mind and decided to go to South Africa because of my trust and respect for connecting with Lisa in the same powerful way that Penny connected with her in San Diego.

" 'Umuntu ngumuntu ngabantu.' Umuntu is translated to mean, 'I am, because you are.' "

—Zulu tribe

We are both in agreement that our journey to South Africa has been one of the most pleasant and well-rounded experiences in our lives. Upon arrival in this vast wilderness, we immediately witnessed a live-action movie scene featuring two mating ostriches. Our guides (who grew up and have lived in Africa their entire lives) said they had never witnessed that before.

The most powerful jewel that came from our South African journey is expressed in three inspiring words: "Umuntu ngumuntu ngabantu." Umuntu is translated to mean, "I am, because you are." The entire Zulu tribe phrase, "Umuntu ngumuntu ngabantu" means that a person is a person through other people.

When we learned about this concept, we understood the meaning of encounters like the one Lisa had at Barbara De Angelis' retreat. We also realized that as you build relationship equity by increasing the quality of your relationships, you are building amazing circles and communities with others and are becoming "a person through other people."

We both knew that the desire to connect with others was far more powerful than either of us had ever been taught! It was fascinating to learn that scientist Matthew Lieberman has done some extensive work in uncovering the neuroscience of human connection and the broad implications for how we live our lives.

Lieberman makes a case to help us understand that our need to connect is as fundamental as our need for food and water. You may be wondering just how powerful and real our need is to connect with one another. There are cultural differences that affect whether and how we connect with others versus how we strive for independence.

We challenge you to take a look at the countless relationships you have formed thus far in your life and examine the ways we are taught to strive for independence. This push for independence may cause you and others to not allow yourself to receive the gift of connection while building community relationships.

The real truth is that when you allow the connection from one soul to another, you open the opportunity for enrichment and positive energy to fuel you. We have heard it said that with a keen sense of awareness, "You are one handshake away from an entirely different lifestyle." This quote says it all. The handshakes, acquaintances, colleagues, bosses, friends, and intimate relationships that we encounter offer the opportunity to dramatically impact our lives! The opportunity for this handshake theory to impact your life is squashed if you refuse to live into the perspective that we are all designed to be relational beings.

Lieberman also points out that languages from around the world use pain language to express social pain. He notes that we say things like, "She broke my heart" or "My feelings were crushed by him." You will gain much value in understanding that social pain is real pain. Lieberman says that social pain and pleasure are wired into our operating system and are motivational ends in and of themselves.

FMRI (Functional Magnetic Resonance Imaging) works by detecting the changes in blood oxygenation and flow that occur in response to neural activity. Research shows that there are two distinct networks in the brain that support social and non-social thinking, and that as one network increases its activity, the other quiets down. These two distinct networks operate like a neural seesaw. Whenever we finish doing non-social thinking, a reflex of social thinking activates immediately.

Lieberman notes that science has recently shown that during quiet moments, the brain is actually preparing to focus on the minds of other people—or to "see the world through a social lens." This clearly proves that our desires and need to connect socially are hardwired into us. We are social creatures by nature!

Social psychologists have done studies noting that the more active the medial prefrontal region of the brain is when someone is trying to persuade you of something, the more likely you'll buy into what they are saying and change your thoughts in agreement.

Our brains don't function like a steel vault that separates us from others. Research by social psychologists suggests that the self is more of a Trojan horse, letting in the beliefs of others without us realizing it.

Society's influence on the individual helps to ensure that we'll have the same kind of beliefs and values as the people around us, and this is a great catalyst for building social harmony. Understanding the impact of how we are hardwired to be social animals helps us embrace the full power of the Umuntu factor.

Umuntu has its roots in humanist African philosophy, where the idea of community is one of the building blocks of society. Umuntu is that nebulous concept of common humanity, oneness: humanity, you, and me. We have embraced this inspiring concept and often pair it up with building unity with our inspirational audiences from around the world, simply saying, "Together we are better." When we share this quote with audiences and participants during our leadership and communication workshops and keynotes, we mean it!

We have never lived into a more powerful set of three words (Umuntu ngumuntu ngabantu) in our lives. We are who we are because of the amazing connections we have made with others on a global scale. Kelly Connery is one of those amazing connections that changed our lives. Kelly played a key role in creating the opportunity for us to match up with and create a lifetime relationship with one of the best spirits on the planet, Lelia Friedlander.

Lisa met Lelia in 2015 when she joined the National Association of Women Business Owners (NAWBO). Lisa says, "The moment we looked into each other's eyes, it was a divine connection. It was reminiscent of that exceptional energetic and magical mutual exchange I shared with Penny in San Diego, California."

It truly was supernatural, and we will never lose touch with such a beautiful soul as Lelia. Lelia blessed us with the connection to her husband, Frank; mother, Miki; father, Tom; and children, Jake and Katie. We hit the mother lode with this amazing family, and Frank is a constant flow of positive energy. He knows how to create and have fun with the best of them! We treasure our connection with all of them.

Lelia is clearly Lisa's sister soul mate. Lisa relates how they met: "We were both asked to co-chair the membership board in our organization. We were in the middle of growing our membership drive and our president, Christy, challenged us to double it in six weeks. We thought this was a ridiculous goal, yet we said we were both up for the challenge.

We were determined to team up and find a way to be even more successful. Lelia and I met and came up with a strategy to go to local woman-owned businesses. We would hold a red-carpet event where each of their businesses would be highlighted at the end with a scavenger hunt, which led all participants through each of their stores with incentives to purchase at discounted rates.

It was extremely important for Lelia and I to put our own business roles on hold for six weeks, and we hit the ground running. With my sales background and Lelia's business acumen, we partnered with thirty businesses. At the end of the six weeks, Lelia and I more than doubled our membership (from 40 to 85 members). How we left one another and those business partners feeling reflected the best principles of the How You Leave Them Feeling concept. We were all full of joy!

Later that year, Lelia and I went to a National Association of Women Business Owners (NAWBO) conference in San Antonio, Texas. Based on our stellar results, we were both recognized and asked to sit down with other NAWBO chapters from around the country and share our success story of how we pulled off this amazing accomplishment.

It had never been done in NAWBO's forty-year history. We both felt this was clearly the Umuntu factor working in our lives! Thanks to Lelia and with Jesse's support at home and in work, we were able to pull it off.

You may ask yourself, 'How do I create these great relationships?' It is the vibration and flow of the energy source. All of this creates great energy right from the start. Ask yourself if this feels like an authentic and real connection and one that is worth pursuing.

You can tap into your intuition. Perhaps you aren't sure how to tap into your intuition. This is the ability to have great perception and quick insights. This is also a feeling you sense in your stomach, as we explained earlier. If your gut is queasy or you have a knot in your stomach, this is your intuition letting you know that something is not right.

You can feel if the connection is real or fake, authentic or inauthentic. You can learn how to tap into it by being aware of it and practicing daily to make it stronger. This can be an invaluable resource. Keep surrounding yourself with people who inspire that automatic connection."

Summary Points

The Umuntu Factor

1. Words are so important in relationships. This Zulu South African phrase ignites community and legions of people in three simple words: "Umuntu ngumuntu ngabantu." This is translated to mean a person is a person through other people.

2. Umuntu is the concept of common humanity, oneness: humanity, you, and me. We have embraced this inspiring concept and often pair it up with building unity with our inspirational audiences, simply saying, "Together we are better."

3. Great relationship connections have the power to enlighten and reshape your life and the lives of others. We like to say "Be mindful that we are all one handshake away from an entirely different life."

Key Action Steps

The Umuntu Factor

1. Whenever you form amazing connections with others that unlock something great inside you, never let go. Stay in touch so that you don't lose those connections!

2. Be mindful of the energy you are putting out. Ensure that you aren't emitting negative energy, creating a negative vibration and an unwanted flow of communication. It is the positive vibration and flow that creates great energy right from the start.

3. Work to have great perception and quick insights. Learn to trust your intuition, which can be felt by that moving feeling in your stomach. Use the power of Umuntu ngumuntu ngabantu to build your best life now!

Chapter 5

The Relationship Excellence Suite: Portfolio

In order to ensure that we include measurable structure in our quest for Relationship Excellence, we designed a Relationship Excellence Suite to house the key components that would offer a roadmap to sustainable and measurable success. We will cover the various components over the next few chapters consisting of the following:

1. 5-Star What Matters Most Assessment
2. House Rules
3. Color Code Personality Assessment
4. The Five Love Languages
5. Relationship Games

"Communication is the solvent of all problems and is the foundation for personal development."

—Peter Shepherd

As we start to unpack the five key Relationship Excellence Suite sections, we'll reintroduce the 5-Star What Matters Most Assessment. This is the basis of understanding yourself and aligning your behaviors so you can relate to others in a clear and meaningful way.

Lisa and I meet weekly to discuss the different components of working on ourselves and the continuous leveling up of our relationship simultaneously.

Besides following my gut instincts as mentioned in Chapter 1, Hyrum Smith's book titled *What Mattters Most* was the key that opened the door to discovering what I wanted. We will take you on a personal deep dive into how our 5-Star What Matters Most Assessment impacted our relationship.

Our 5-Star What Matters Most Assessment allowed me to define my values and take a closer look at the roles being played and those that weren't being played at the 5-Star importance rating level and at the

5-Star performance rating level. Please see our 5-Star What Matters Most Assessment below:

Level of Importance Rating

5 Stars: Most important
4 Stars: Important
3 Stars: Moderately important
2 Stars: Not too important
1 Star: Noteworthy

We also use this rating system to rank and qualify how well we are performing with developing, servicing, and enrolling our values and roles. Please see our 5-Star performance rating system below:

Level of Performance Rating

5 Stars: Excellent
4 Stars: Good
3 Stars: Fair
2 Stars: Not Good
1 Star: Poor

5-Star What Matters Most Assessment – Roles Phase I

1. List your most important roles
2. Using a 5-Star rating system, rate how important your roles are to you
3. Rate the performance of how well you are living into your roles
4. Write a brief description of why your roles are important to you
5. Group your roles based on similarity

5-Star What Matters Most Assessment –
Values Phase II

1. List your most important values
2. Using a 5-Star rating system, rate how important your values are to you
3. Rate the performance of how well you are living into your values
4. Write a brief description of why your values are important to you
5. Group your values based on similarity

See a completed 5-Star What Matters Most Assessment showcasing grouped roles and values below:

5-STAR WHAT MATTERS MOST ASSESSMENT—ROLES PHASE I

Count	Importance Level (0–5 stars)	Individual Roles	Performance Rating (0–5 stars)	Roles Sorted by Group
1	4.0	Chameleon	4.0	
2	4.0	Entertainer	3.0	
3	4.5	Humility	4.5	
4	5.0	Inspirer	4.0	**Character Role**
5	4.5	Listener	3.0	**8 Roles**
6	4.0	Peacemaker	3.0	
7	4.0	Role Model	3.0	
8	4.5	Transcending Race	4.0	
	4.3		**3.6**	
9	5.0	Educator	4.0	
10	5.0	Learner (Student)	3.0	**Educational Role 3 Roles**
11	4.5	Reader	3.0	
	4.8		**3.3**	
12	4.0	Friend	3.0	
13	5.0	Husband	2.0	
14	5.0	Problem Solver	3.0	**Personal Relationships Role 5 Roles**
15	4.0	Family Relative	2.0	
16	5.0	Relationship Manager	3.0	
	4.6		**2.6**	
17	4.0	Business Owner	4.0	
18	4.5	Coach	4.0	
19	4.5	Experienced Marketer	2.0	**Professional Role 5 Roles**
20	4.0	Inspirational Leader & Speaker	3.0	
21	4.0	Partner	2.0	
	4.2		**3.0**	

Average Importance Level
4.5

Average Performance Rating
3.1

5-STAR WHAT MATTERS MOST ASSESSMENT—VALUES PHASE II

Count	Individual Governing Values	Value Rating	Governing Values Sorted by Priority and Group	Performance Rating	My Governing Values Statements and Why They Are Important To Me
1	Mental Health	5.0	**Health 3 Values**	1.5	Being mentally healthy allows me the proper mindset to work through or resolve all life matters in good spirit
2	Physical Health	5.0		3.0	Maintaining good physical health gives me positive energy to live out a full range of unconstricting life choices
3	Spiritual Health	5.0		2.0	Being spiritually connected allows me to accept, learn, and live from unseen sources
		5.0		**2.2**	
4	Faithfulness	5.0	**Authentic 7 Values**	1.0	Faithfulness demonstrates your desire to be respectful and truthful to those that have agreements with
5	Honesty	5.0		3.0	It allows others to build trust and offers communication and intention that they can count on
6	Integrity	5.0		3.0	Integrity is couched in consistently doing what I have committed to do
7	Peace of Mind	5.0		2.0	Good peace of mind allows me to live peacefully in my own skin
8	Personal Responsibility	4.0		2.0	Personal responsibility is a measure of taking full ownership while remaining accountable
9	Intuition	4.0		3.5	Tapping into intuition allows me to get in touch with my inner guiding system, using instincts to guide me
10	Time (the value and usage of time)	5.0		3.5	Time is the most precious commodity; it's perishable and invaluable, I honor, respect and use it wisely
		4.7		**2.6**	
11	Equality	4.5	**Open-Minded 3 Values**	2.0	Nobody is left out based on prejudice
12	Level Playing Field	4.5		2.0	Everyone has a chance at winning
13	Opportunity	5.0		3.0	The only shot at winning is by having opportunity to get in the game
		4.7		**2.3**	

Count	Individual Governing Values	Value Rating	Governing Values Sorted by Priority and Group	Performance Rating	My Governing Values Statements and Why They Are Important To Me
14	Care	4.0		4.0	Care is important as it feeds a positive nature and investment into my relationships
15	Compassion	4.0		4.0	Showing compassion adds value to my relationships allowing others to receive my support
16	Empathy	4.0		4.0	Empathy helps to understand where others are coming from and allows me to relate to them
17	Generosity	4.0		4.0	Being generous leaves me feeling good to know that I'm helping others in their time of need or want
18	Giving	4.0	Contribution 11 Values	4.0	Giving brings me great pleasure and demonstrates the depth of my care, it leaves me feeling good
19	Love	5.0		4.0	Love is one of the deepest most positive emotions that touches us in a range of ways
20	Self-preservation	5.0		2.0	Valuing self-preservation proves that we care and love ourselves enough to matter and continue striving for our best progression
21	Service	5.0		4.0	Good service is largely well received and most people value and appreciate it
22	Sharing	4.0		2.0	Sharing allows a blissful exchange of important information and resources
23	Supporting Key Relationships	4.0		2.0	Supporting key relationships brings pleasure on all sides
24	The Power of Words	5.0		3.0	Respecting the power of words allows me to leave people and situations better than I found them

Average Value Rating

4.4

4.7

Average Performance Rating

3.4

2.6

Once all the values and roles are grouped and ranked, we then look to see if we are in full alignment with our values in relationship to our roles.

As an example, if you rated both your role as a husband and the value of integrity with five stars each, yet you were cheating on your wife, your roles and values would be out of alignment.

The 5-Star What Matters Most Assessment is a way to help people clarify their priorities and best actions. When you consistently act in contrast to your values, you remain out of alignment and will experience a feeling of "something wrong" in your gut. This can become your normal behavior and you can actually lose track of how out of balance you are.

You may tend to make yourself feel like everything is okay when it truly isn't. You must learn to consistently leave yourself feeling well in order to live the life you deserve and desire!

Using our 5-Star What Matters Most Assessment helps you do what Anthony Ciccone, President of Ciccone McKay Financial Group in Vancouver, Canada, calls "A check-up, from the neck up." When your values and roles are in a positive full alignment with your actions, this is the foundation for building and living into a life by design!

"A check up from the neck up."

—Anthony Ciccone

For more than twenty-one years, we have amassed a host of case studies and testimonials from the personal and professional development clients who have created a positive transformation in their close relationships by using our 5-Star What Matters Most Assessment. It was awesome to learn that they were able to remove their fears, difficulties, and unresolved matters within their most intimate relationships.

James Cleveland, a professional clinical counselor and marriage and family therapist, was one of our clients who has an amazing story that he has given us the permission to share. His story helps others get a vivid picture of the power of getting into alignment with your behavior and life choices through the close examination of your roles and values.

James rated integrity and family at a high, 5-Star level. However, in terms of how James was showing up in his role in his family grouping, the level was about two stars.

James realized that his failure to make decisions was not only keeping him in a broken relationship with his wife, but also preventing him from moving on to a healthy, intimate relationship and from spending quality time with his family. He was out of alignment.

On his occasional gut checks, James knew in his stomach that something needed to change, but he had no idea what to change or even where to start looking at what needed to change in his life. Before participating on our coaching program and making the connections on our 5-Star What Matters Most Assessment, he was lost, broken, and slipping quickly down into a rotten cesspool!

Following the completion of his 5-Star What Matters Most Assessment and some internal discovery work evaluating his choices and lack of choices, James became very intentional about making the tough decisions to restore inner peace, joy, and alignment back into his life.

James credits his participation and execution with getting clear with his important values and roles as the keys to unlocking how to live his life by design from a foundational level. I personally had a similar experience when I created my 5-Star What Matters Most Assessment.

When I realized my family roles and personal values were out of alignment, it was an eye-opening showstopper! I had to move from anxiety, embarrassment, guilt, shame, blame, and apathy to a life by design based on my strongest values and roles. Some of my top roles and values at that time were:

Values	Roles
Time	Significant Other
Power of the word	Business Owner
Honor	Life Coach
Integrity	Leader
Creativity	Inspirational Speaker

My new 5-Star What Matters Most Assessment was my "plan-before-the-plan" system, tool, and process. The "plan-before-the-plan" is a concept of creating a strategy of gathering all of the critical components before you start the planning development phase. This is when the tough work began! Daily use of this new system was the key to unlocking the door and rebuilding a quality life. My top relationships were now based on living into my best values, while up-leveling my roles.

Regardless of whether you are facing an inevitable divorce or the destruction of a personal friendship, intimate relationship, or business partnership, adhering to the use of our 5-Star What Matters Most Assessment will be life-changing! Our 5-Star What Matters Most Assessment was created to connect your gut instincts, intuition, and truth-based reality with the opportunity for rebuilding a solid foundation toward the reconstruction of living into your best life…by design!

This concept turns on bright lights during extremely dark times! It offers a breath of clarity and direction that you may be craving. When you elevate yourself and your behavior by working through your 5-Star What Matters

Most Assessment, it sets up the opportunity for building relationship equity with yourself and others.

Summary Points

The Relationship Excellence Suite:
5-Star What Matters Most Assessment

1. The 5-Star What Matters Most Assessment is a way to help people clarify their priorities and their best actions. When you consistently act in contrast to your values, you remain out of alignment and will experience a feeling of "something wrong" in your gut. This can become your normal behavior, and you can actually lose track of how out of balance you are.

2. Values and roles are ranked according to a five-star rating system, where five represents the highest priority and values, while one represents those of lowest importance. Ranking your values in this way clearly shows what is most important to you.

3. Working through your 5-Star What Matters Most Assessment sets up the opportunity for building relationship equity with yourself and others.

Key Action Steps

The Relationship Excellence Suite:
What Matters Most Portfolio

1. Make a list of the five values that are most important to you as a person and also list the five most important roles you play in your life. Examples are father, mother, business owner, dog owner, life partner, etc.

2. Rate your values with the numbers one through five, with five being most important and one being the least important.

3. Study the values and roles you have listed and determine whether your key values are aligned with your behaviors and decisions in real life.

If you find yourself out of alignment between your highest roles and values, take the time to determine exactly what action steps you must take in order to bring yourself back into alignment.

Chapter 6

The Relationship Excellence Suite: Color Code Personality Assessment

Taylor Hartman, PhD, invented the Color Code Personality Assessment. The Color Code divides personalities into four colors based on the idea that all people possess one of four Driving Core Motives (DCM), which is an understanding of what you do and why you do it. The Color Code focuses on helping you understand your character at the innate level— the unique character that you were born with. This accurate knowledge helps you gain much deeper and more useful insights into what makes you and those around you tick.

When you remain open to receiving cues and behavior signals from others, it puts you in a position of being able to effectively understand their Driving Core Motives. The next step beyond understanding the DCM of others would be to communicate and respond to others in a relatable fashion. Their DCM represent clear distinctions of their dominant disposition.

We call this the process of learning to speak the language of others. When others feel like you understand them and can relate to them in the way they most desire, it raises your communication to the highest level. It can be likened to establishing a good rhythm or flow while communicating with others.

Choosing to elevate the power of communication is a real game changer and puts you far ahead of the pack. It puts you in a rare category of relating and communicating well with others that are not like yourself.

The Color Code has been a game changer in my and Lisa's relationship and in our ability to quickly connect with others. We understand one another on a personality and communication level. We literally speak one another's language, and we have chosen to learn how to speak the language of others as well.

Speaking the language of others offers you the tools to communicate in a way they will quickly understand. This quick understanding happens because you are communicating with an intention to adjust how you engage with others in order to connect with their Driving Core Motives. We call this 'meeting them where they are' during communication.

Summary of The Four Core Colors
Obtained with permission from Color Code, LLC

In the following summary, be mindful that rather than choosing other-naming features to describe the Driving Core Motives distinctions, the representation of the blue, red, yellow, and white colors is more practical and memorable. These four colors depict what traits a person has and how those traits correspond with their overall personality.

BLUES (DCM is Intimacy)
What does it mean to be motivated by intimacy as a Blue?

Being motivated by intimacy means that Blues like to connect with others on a deep and meaningful level. Just ask any Blue how they feel about people who are fake/superficial, and you will get quite a strong reaction.

Blues want nothing to do with those kinds of people because intimacy for a Blue is about truth, legitimacy, integrity, loyalty, and sincerity. Most Blues will tell you that they can count the number of their true friends on one hand because those are the people with whom they feel that real, intimate connection.

Blues need to be understood and appreciated. Everything they do is quality-based. They are loyal friends, employers, and employees. Whatever or whomever they commit to is their sole (and soul) focus. They love to serve and give of themselves freely in order to nurture others' lives.

Blues have distinct preferences and have the most controlling personality. Their personal code of ethics is remarkably strong and they expect others to live honest, committed lives as well. They enjoy sharing meaningful moments in conversation as well as paying close attention to special life events like birthdays and anniversaries.

Blues are dependable, thoughtful, and analytical, but can also be self-righteous, worry-prone, and moody. When you deal with Blues, be sincere and make a genuine effort to understand and appreciate them.

WHITES (DCM is Peace)
What does it mean to be motivated
by peace as a White?

While it is true that most Whites are not typically big fans of conflict, their definition of peace runs deeper than simply the absence of conflict. To a White, peace is all about inner harmony and balance.

They don't like to have that equilibrium disrupted. That's why they try to change the subject if you attempt to talk about something that makes them feel insecure. They don't want to stir things up inside.

They seek independence and require kindness. They resist confrontation at all costs. To them, feeling good is more important than being good. They are typically quiet by nature and process things very deeply and objectively with great clarity.

Of all the colors, Whites are the best listeners. They respect people who are direct, but recoil from perceived hostility or verbal battle. Whites need their alone time and they refuse to be controlled by others. They want to do things their own way and in their own time. They ask little of others and resent others demanding much of them.

Whites are much stronger than people think, but are not often seen for their strength because they don't easily reveal their feelings. Whites are even-tempered, diplomatic, and the voice of reason, but can also be indecisive, unexpressive, and silently stubborn. When you deal with Whites, be kind, accept and support their individuality, and look for nonverbal clues to understand their feelings.

REDS (DCM is Power)
What does it mean to be motivated
by power as a Red?

Sometimes people think about power in terms of control. While it's true that Reds like to be in control of their circumstances and are attracted to leadership opportunities, that's not a very complete picture of what power really means to Reds. To Reds, power generally means the ability to move from point A to point B— and to do it in the most direct and efficient way possible.

The Spanish and Portuguese translation for the word "power" as a verb is "poder" which means, "to be able to do." That is a very fitting description of what power means to a Red. They want to be productive and efficient.

They seek productivity and need to look good to others. Simply stated, Reds want their own way. They like to be in the driver's seat and willingly pay the price to be in a leadership role.

Reds value whatever gets them ahead in life, whether it is in their careers, school endeavors, or personal life. What Reds value, they get done. They are often workaholics. They will, however, resist doing anything that doesn't interest them.

Reds like to be right. They value approval from others for their intelligence and practical approach to life and want to be respected for it. Reds are confident, proactive, and visionary, but can also be arrogant, selfish, and insensitive. When you deal with Reds, be precise, factual, direct, and show no fear.

YELLOWS (DCM is Fun)
What does it mean to be motivated
by fun as a Yellow?

Fun does not simply mean that Yellows are seeking endless frivolity and that they never take things seriously.

People incorrectly assume that Yellows don't like structure, when in fact, they crave it. It only looks like they resist it because most Yellows don't know how to create structure on their own. Fun to a Yellow actually means "living in the moment."

It means that they enjoy the process of what they are doing far more than the end result. That's why Yellows are generally so engaged and "present" when you are with them. They are focused on the here and now and nothing else. Carpe diem or "seize the day" is a Yellow way of life.

Yellows are inviting and embrace life as a party that they're hosting. They love playful interaction and can be extremely sociable. They are highly persuasive and seek instant gratification. Yellows need to be adored and praised. While Yellows are carefree, they are sensitive and highly alert to others' agendas to control them. Yellows typically carry a good heart.

Yellows need to look good socially, and friendships command a high priority in their lives. Yellows are happy, articulate, engaging of others, and crave adventure. Easily distracted, they can never sit still for long. They embrace each day in the present tense and choose to be around people who, like themselves, enjoy a curious nature.

Yellows are charismatic, spontaneous, and positive, but can also be irresponsible, obnoxious, and forgetful. When you deal with Yellows, take a positive, upbeat approach and promote light-hearted, creative, and fun interactions.

See the chart on the following page for a brief quick reference of the four core colors.

	RED:	BLUE:	WHITE:	YELLOW:
CORE MOTIVE	Power	Intimacy	Peace	Fun
NATURAL TALENTS	Leadership Vision	Quality Service	Clarity Tolerance	Enthusiasm Optimism

You will gain enormous value in applying the Color Code and learning about your DCM. Exploring your Color Code assessment results and the makeup and breakdown of your DCM will be a real game changer in your life.

Should you choose to take the Color Code personality assessment and you want to start enrolling this intelligence into the power of how you communicate with others, start by using the four core colors chart above. This can be your guiding light on how to speak to each of the four colors during communication.

The breakdown of the Driving Core Motives for all four colors gives you a great understanding of this people-science tool and how to understand others. It starts with you. The Color Code philosophy is, "When you get self, you get others." Basically, this translates into knowing that when you start to understand yourself and your distribution of the four colors, you will understand others better because they also have some level of representation of all four colors in their Driving Core Motives.

Part of the Color Code is a full report that identifies your wants and needs, your strengths and limitations, and a strategy to increase the attraction of your personality and communication style. We feel enormous gratitude for the countless lives that we have touched throughout the years using this tool with our clients. The ripple effect on families, intimate relationships, and countless leadership teams, associations, small businesses, and entrepreneurs is astounding.

How many of your relationships could you improve if you learned how to fully understand the wants and needs as well as the Driving Core Motives of self and others?

In order to take the Color Code personality assessment, please email us at LisaListen9@jesstalk.com and remember to place "Color Code Request" in the subject line.

Lisa and I have chosen to add a Color Code accountability partnership pillar to our relationship. This allows us to help remove our limiting characteristics while demonstrating our character strengths. This concept helps us speak one another's language and the language of others fluently.

I learned a great example of speaking Lisa's language after she took the Color Code personality assessment. I originally believed that our characters and personalities were the same. After studying her Color Code results, I learned that our innate characters weren't exactly the same. Lisa's core color of white had the characteristic of always seeking inner peace and not liking to deal with conflict or confrontation.

This was a real eye-opening lesson for me to learn about Lisa. I changed my style of communicating with Lisa to offer more opportunity for her to take the time that she required to process matters, rather than insisting on immediate feedback during conversations. Yes, I chose to learn how to speak her language, not assuming that she was exactly like me and wanted to communicate in the style that I prefer.

This is a common mistake that many people make regarding communication. Did you learn that old saying, "Treat others how you want to be treated?" Learning and enrolling the Color Code has taught us that in order to elevate the quality of your relationships, it's best to "Treat others how they want to be treated." This is such a simple communication standard, and we witness that it is rarely used by others.

When you receive your results after submitting your answers to the Color Code personality assessment, you will also learn your innate strengths and limitations, needs and wants, and your secondary color. In addition to heightening your self-awareness, this report will give you insights and suggestions for creating more successful and rewarding personal and professional relationships.

Lisa and I chose to stop treating one another the way we want to be treated. Instead, we learned how to understand the innate character of one another, advancing and living the strategy of treating others how they want to be treated. We call this type of relationship communication continuous development.

To see the differences and similarities in our Color Code results summary, find below an example of the character strengths we want to showcase and the limitations we have chosen to remove. We practice speaking one another's language while working to ensure we get it right consistently!

Lisa & Jesse Character Strengths

Lisa's Strengths	Jesse's Strengths
Diplomatic	Quality-Oriented
Good Listener	Nurturing
Even Tempered	Dependable
Compassionate	Leader
Intuitive	Creative Thinker

Lisa & Jesse Character Limitations

Lisa's Limitations	Jesse's Limitations
Detached	Emotionally Intense
Unexpressive	Perfectionist
Silently Stubborn	Unrealistic Expectations
Avoids Conflict	Calculating
Reluctant	Self-Critical

For an even more comprehensive comparison, see an example of Lisa and Jesse's Color Code results below:

Lisa & Jesse Color Code Results

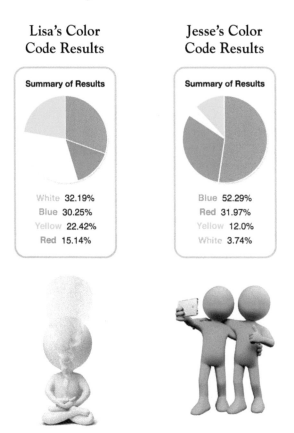

Lisa's Color Code Results

Summary of Results

White 32.19%
Blue 30.25%
Yellow 22.42%
Red 15.14%

Jesse's Color Code Results

Summary of Results

Blue 52.29%
Red 31.97%
Yellow 12.0%
White 3.74%

Your second largest color wedge in your pie chart is typically referred to as your secondary. Most people have a primary and secondary that represents why they do what they do.

The combination of these two areas makes up the largest portion of your character, and your personality and character are shaped by these two large pieces of your Color Code pie chart. There are also Color Code purists. These are people who have such a large wedge of pie in their core color that they don't have a secondary color. The character and behavior of purists are typically highly identifiable and consistent. You will get a better understanding of how two Color Code purists show up in the following story featuring our clients, Pamela and Willie Mae.

During our personal and professional leadership coaching program with Pamela and Willie Mae, it became very evident that neither of them would allow the other to express an alternative perspective on important matters. So, it was no surprise when the Color Code revealed that Pamela was a yellow purist, and Willie Mae was a blue purist.

The character and behavior of purists are typically highly identifiable and consistent because of the dominating percentages lodged in the driving core motive of one color. The nice thing about communicating with purists is that because their core color is such a vast segment of their DCM pie chart result, you know precisely their driving core motive.

The flip side to the purist character is that because their core color is so dominant, they don't have a secondary color to natively kick in as needed to relate to other colors' character strengths. Not having a secondary color can make purists inflexible to connecting to the characteristics of different colors and challenging to get along with whenever you disagree with their perspective. They don't see additional clear or helpful views other than their own.

We encountered these business partners that were both purists, and they couldn't even see the transparent and prudent perspectives of one another. Examine the predominant make-up of each of their strengths and limitations below:

Willie Mae & Pamela Character Strengths

Willie Mae's Strengths
Quality-Oriented
Detail-Conscious
Intuitive
Deliberate
Intuitive

Pamela's Strengths
Spontaneous
Charismatic
Happy
Sociable
Forgiving

Willie Mae & Pamela Character Limitations

Willie Mae's Limitations
Guilt Prone
Jealous
Moody
Unforgiving
Worry Prone

Pamela's Limitations
Disorganized
Forgetful
Inconsistent
Undisciplined
Unfocused

The detailed report on the following page will give you more insight into each of their characters. Pamela is a 67.52% yellow purist, which means that she is motivated by fun, and she likes to keep matters very light.

Yellows enjoy the process of what they are doing far more than the result. Yellows are generally so engaged and "present" when you are with them. They are focused on the here and now and nothing else.

Blues are motivated by intimacy. As a Blue, being inspired by intimacy means that they like to connect with others on a deep and meaningful level. Willie Mae is a 68.21% blue, and she is motivated by being understood. For an even more comprehensive comparison, see Willie Mae and Pamela's Color Code results below:

Pamela & Willie Mae Color Code Results

Pamela's Color Code Results

Willie Mae's Color Code Results

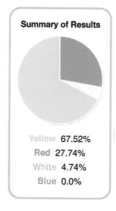

Summary of Results

Yellow 67.52%
Red 27.74%
White 4.74%
Blue 0.0%

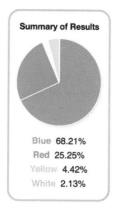

Summary of Results

Blue 68.21%
Red 25.25%
Yellow 4.42%
White 2.13%

Pamela was naturally fun-loving with a kind heart. She chose not to attend a university or college following graduation from high school and started working in the field of marketing at an early age. Everybody was drawn to Pamela, and she never had a shortage of friends.

Willie Mae's character was the polar opposite of Pamela. She graduated from a Southern university with high marks, majoring in marketing. She pushed very aggressively to be understood and found it difficult to maintain friendships.

Pamela and Willie Mae were introduced at a special event focusing on the dynamics of marketing. The two of them originally hit it off and decided to go into business together. They chose to become entrepreneurs and build a company together in the field of marketing.

These entrepreneurs came to us because they were at an absolute impasse in terms of being able to understand one another or communicate effectively. They couldn't hear the words the other spoke and constantly interrupted each other with their own viewpoints. It was extremely difficult to play the role of personal and professional coach during such chaotic and caustic communication. We valued being able to bring our wide-ranging experience to assisting these entrepreneurs in growing their communication style with one another.

Their multilevel marketing company was failing miserably after an early run of success. We were faced with helping these two entrepreneurs find a way to understand one another and learn to communicate at a very foundational and basic level.

We didn't see progress in their ability to communicate effectively until we encouraged them to take the Color Code personality assessment. They were both dumbfounded when they received and shared their results. Pamela had no idea that Willie Mae could not relate to her light-hearted nature. Willie Mae was astonished that Pamela didn't value her strong desire to deep dive into every matter with maximum care and understanding.

Willie Mae and Pamela allowed us to focus our coaching sessions on breaking down their results and choosing which limitations to remove while upholding and building positive character strengths with them. This was the first step in helping them work more cohesively together as professional partners.

In order to ensure they gained the highest value from coaching and what they learned from the Color Code Personality Assessment would stick, we followed up with a Business Rules & Practical Intelligence Agreement. This was a pledge where agreed-upon business practices and common sense must be adhered to by both partners.

The Color Code coaching sessions fostered the opportunity of turning negative communication into positive communication while practical intelligence was helping them accept, embrace, and enroll the practice of using common sense consistently. Did you know that common sense isn't so common? This partnership represented the most difficult coaching relationship Lisa and I had seen in our twenty-two years of coaching.

"If you argue for your limitations, they are yours."

—Dr. Taylor Hartman

If we didn't have the brilliant tool of the Color Code Personality Assessment, we wouldn't have been able to help these emotionally challenged leaders. Most of us find it very difficult to make the prudent changes in our lives. We tend to hold onto our limitations even when we know they are costing us valuable relationship points and untold opportunities. Dr. Taylor Hartman, the author and creator of the Color Code, says it best: "If you argue for your limitations, they are yours."

It is one thing to take on something like the Color Code, and it is an entirely different matter to learn the truth about how to up-level your communication style, remove limitations, learn new character strengths and character development while sticking with the process through change and transformation. When you make the choice to do the work while respecting the process, you gain the opportunity to reinforce the importance of support and structure in order to change.

We trust you noticed the concepts of the Color Code—learning the language of others—and understanding others' Driving Core Motives come together as the essence of How You Leave Them Feeling. It is through simply being mindful of others and making adjustments that you create inspiring love, relationships, and connection.

Summary Points

The Relationship Excellence Suite: Color Code Personality Assessment

1. The Color Code Personality Assessment divides personalities into four colors. The main idea behind the Color Code is that all people possess one of four Driving Core Motives (DCM).

2. The Color Code focuses on helping you understand yourself at the innate level. You will learn the character that you have innately been born into. It also focuses on helping you discover your DCM, which translates to an understanding of what you do and why you do it.

3. Understanding your DCM using the Color Code Personality Assessment helps you increase the quality of your character and improve your ability to communicate and connect with others regardless of their Driving Core Motives.

Key Action Steps

The Relationship Excellence Suite: Color Code Personality Assessment

1. Take the Color Code Personality Assessment in order to understand yourself at an innate level and understand how to communicate with others in the way they prefer. The goal is to not only start speaking your language better, but to learn to speak the language of others efficiently.

2. Once you take the Color Code Personality Assessment, ensure that you read your full Color Code report and determine which of your limitations you are going to eliminate and which of your strengths you will highlight when communicating with others. You can receive a Color Code report by contacting us at LisaListen9@jesstalk.com and requesting to take the Color Code personality assessment.

3. When you are ready to do the work, get an accountability partner who you spend a considerable amount of time with. Allow them to be a solid witness for you becoming healthy and charactered by Color Code standards.

In order to start applying the Color Code intelligence in your communication with others, use the detailed Color Code descriptions and illustrations in this chapter as a guiding light to speak to their DCM.

Chapter 7

The Relationship Excellence Suite: House Rules, Love Languages, and Games

The final breakdown of the Relationship Excellence Suite is designed to develop and promote synergy, engagement, and joy in your essential and intimate relationships. These components can assist individuals, couples, business partners, and friends in improving their day-to-day interactions and increasing positivity and connection. We'll cover those final Relationship Excellence Suite components in this chapter.

House Rules

Early on in my and Lisa's relationship, we had a conversation about the large number of couples that we've met who didn't have a rhythm of how to live together in a harmonious fashion. Each of their personal wants and needs would drive the other nuts, and the other partner largely ignored those wants and needs.

As we studied this phenomenon and reflected on our own past relationships, we quickly realized that neither of us had ever experienced this elusive harmony. The truth is that we made the same mistakes that countless other had made – we never established any agreements regarding our specific wants and needs in our own relationships.

This was a defining moment, and we decided to right this wrong that had been handed down through the ages, generation after generation. We vowed that each of us would identify and share a minimum of one and a maximum of three of our strongest desires in order to creat our own harmonious living space.

We created and agreed upon the following ways that this revolutionary way of living would work. Taking the time to create powerful and connected agreements about how we wanted to live felt awesome. We chose to call these agreements House Rules. If you are not fond of subscribing to a rules concept, you may choose to consider them as agreements that you make with one another and call them House Agreements. The terminology of House Agreements works very well because that is exactly what you are establishing: an understanding and agreement of what is best for your and your partner.

House Rules Bylaws

1. Each partner's chosen House Rule is non-negotiable and respected in the exact fashion as designed.
2. Each partner must submit at least one and no more than three House Rules that they request to be respected.
3. You must know and respect one another's House Rules.
4. Every 90 days, all House Rules must be discussed to determine whether you are both honoring and respecting each other's House Rules.
5. You may elect to swap out one or more of your House Rules every 90 days as desired.

One of Lisa's house rules is that she requires the first hour of each new day to spend privately waking up into our world. She uses this time for meditation, tub time, self-discovery, and pondering her strategy for the day.

One of my House Rules is SWITCH. The purpose of SWITCH is to request that any time Lisa sees or feels that I may be doing something or not doing something that is hurting our relationship or business in any manner, she must bring that to my attention.

Once Lisa brings the concern to my attention and asks for a SWITCH moment, regarding the details of this House Rule, the only option I have is to make the SWITCH. I must switch from whatever mindset I currently have to the mindset that she knows will deliver us the winning hand!

On a speaking engagement trip from Vancouver, Canada, to Yosemite, California, I observed a behavior in Lisa that was not allowing her to focus on what mattered most at the moment and was causing a costly disconnect. I then had a lightbulb moment and realized that I was guilty of the same behavior regarding Lisa's insistence that I start asking prospects to become speaking or coaching clients.

My belief system was that as long as I was good enough at what I do, I should not have to ask for the business. I now admit that I couldn't have been more wrong about something that was so important and necessary. This lightbulb moment is where the SWITCH rule was created. The SWITCH concept may be used during important personal matters as well.

The new SWITCH House Rules state that anytime either partner sees the other partner doing something that is either costing them major opportunities or not allowing the wins and gains that are available with the infusion of the right effort, the only thing that the knowing partner has to do is say SWITCH.

The unknowing partner has to verbally say, "I have switched" and make the necessary follow-up moves to honor switching to the logic of the knowing partner.

If the unknowing partner has no clue as to what they are switching, they ask the knowing partner what they are being asked to SWITCH. Once the knowing partner shares what is being requested to SWITCH, the unknowing partner simply says SWITCH.

Lisa and I were preparing for a special speaking engagement for the Word of Life Christian Academy in Las Vegas. We believed quantifying the benefit of this House Rule and sharing it with the students would show them how powerful this tool could be if they honored it in their lives.

We conducted a cost-benefit analysis of all the missed opportunities from ages 16-46. What if I had only started asking for the business as opposed to waiting for prospects to solicit my services? The results were illuminating. What a costly lesson – the earned revenue potential exceeded $135 million! Can you say SWITCH?

The 5 Love Languages

One of the simplest relationship systems, tools, and processes that Lisa and I use is called the 5 Love Languages, a concept developed by Gary Chapman, PhD, author, speaker, and counselor. Everyone gives and receives love differently. Dr. Chapman offers a significant insight into these differences, and you can be confidently equipped to communicate love well by adhering to his 5 Love Languages concept, which are:

1. Acts of service
2. Receiving gifts
3. Quality time
4. Words of affirmation
5. Physical touch

The benefits of identifying someone's love language are inclusive to all relationships: married or dating couples, children and teenagers, friends and coworkers, budding and mature relationships.

You may make the same mistakes that countless others have made regarding how you like to be treated. There's a rule that you may be familiar with called "The Golden Rule," which says to treat others how you like to be treated. This would be simple and easy if everyone else was just like you. Since we are all unique in our own ways, we suggest that you considering learning and adopting "The Platinum Rule." The Platinum Rule recommends that you treat others how they want to be treated…and typically they will tell you! When it comes to your desire to enjoy great intimate relationships, consider how your significant other would like to be treated.

Our current society is over the top with information overload and crazy, busy schedules. When it comes to knowing exactly how to relate to your significant other, business partner, or friend and expressing love in the fashion of their choosing, your best intentions will likely fall by the wayside.

One aspect worth mentioning that can confuse our knowledge of a partner's love language is how comfortable we get in our relationship. Relationship comfort can be a problem when we get so lax with a close or intimate relationship (like we may do with our husbands, wives, parents, girlfriends, boyfriends, best friends, coworkers, bosses, sisters, and brothers) that we take them and their feelings for granted. Relationship comfort can be seen in all close or intimate relationships.

We also take for granted the work that must continue to happen within all relationships, especially our closest relationships. We may forget to be kind, caring,

" 'The Golden Rule,' which says to treat others how you like to be treated."

—*Unknown*

" 'The Platinum Rule.' The Platinum Rule recommends that you treat others how they want to be treated…"

—*Unknown*

supporting, helpful, and responsible. We stop hearing or faithfully listening to the other person. We act like they are always going to be there. Getting too comfortable in a relationship can be like a screen that blocks a beautiful view across the landscape of life.

In an effort to feel connected and in union with others on one side of the screen, we crave and seek to attract the best, closest, and longest-lasting relationships. On the other side of the screen, we may knowingly or unknowingly become blind to our poor behavior in our closest relationships, and that will ultimately sabotage relationship longevity.

Your best avenue to the winner's circle of life is to raise your relationship comfort awareness. Remember to embrace and give continuous value to your most important relationships. Remain mindful in appreciating and nurturing your valued connections with others. Also be mindful of human nature related to forgetting or disrespecting longer-term relationships. Try not to fall into a happenstance attitude of feeling tired of what feels same old and familiar. This reduced awareness is a relationship killer!

Raising your awareness includes simple gestures of appreciation like saying "thank you" and "please." Always remember that it is human nature to become complacent in long-term relationships. We get bored of the same old, same old familiar relationships.

In order to create the best pathways in our closest relationships, we want to embrace the positive side of relationship comfort and be mindful to drop the negative side. Understanding the 5 Love Languages and identifying the language of friends and partners offers additional tools to use to prevent us from falling into the negative side of relationship comfort.

Relationship Games

Our Relationship Excellence Suite is topped off with two games, the first is called Dialogue. This game was designed to be used with couples who want to continue knowing more about one another in conversations that likely wouldn't come about without this game.

Start the game by flipping a coin to determine who goes first. The winner of the coin toss chooses a favorite song from their past, and the partner who is listening to the song has to attempt to guess the artist and name of the song. The partner guessing correctly receives 2.5 points for each correct answer.

The partner who chose the song now tells a compelling story about what was going on in their life during the time period of the chosen song. The partner listening to the song rates the quality of the story from one to five, with five representing a great story. Once the story has been shared and rated by the other partner, you now trade sides and your partner switches to the person choosing the song.

You take turns until you have both chosen two songs. Once this has been completed, total up all the points and determine the winner of your Dialogue game. Ultimately, everyone will walk away with great value from playing this game because you will learn more about your significant other.

Lisa and I love this game and have played with other couples. It always raises the level of connection with the other couples. As you build infectious energy while connecting with others, you will leave them feeling positive, and they will not want to let you go.

Another one of our fun relationship games is called, "Wow—What I Like About You." In this game, we take turns trying to wow one another by doing things that we believe the other will appreciate or enjoy.

Then, we set aside thirty minutes to recall and share the awesome actions and gestures that we have received from one another. This game also uses a scoring system of one to five. Five is the highest wow factor and one is a vote of appreciation.

This game teaches you each other's likes and how best to incorporate those things into your relationship. Once you have played this game, the excitement will encourage you to continue discovering new details about your partner!

Summary Points

Relationships Excellence Suite:
House Rules, Love Languages, and Games

1. Creating House Rules is a way for couples, friends, and business partners to live together with respect. It's identifying and sharing a minimum of one and a maximum of three of our strongest desires of how we want to live in the same space.

2. Understanding which of the five love languages your friend, partner, or spouse prefers is another way to foster respect and raise your relationship up to a higher level. This is an important element in how you leave people feeling.

3. Playing relationship games such as "Dialogue" and "Wow—What I Like about You" is another way to deepen your relationship with others and influence How You Leave Them Feeling. It's a fun addition to family get-togethers or an evening with another couple.

Key Action Steps

Relationships Excellence Suite: House Rules, Love Languages, and Games

1. Don't simply settle for your intimate relationships as they currently are. Make a clear choice to step into relationship excellence by following some of the proven methods and strategies in this chapter.

2. Spend some time determining your own House Rules and write them down on a piece of paper or record them on your iPad. Make sure they represent what is truly most important to you.

3. Do you know your own love language? Do you know your partner's love language? See if you can figure it out and then discuss your ideas with your partner or friend.

Chapter 8

Friendship, Love, and Marriage:
Those Special Bonds

There are countless ways to determine the meaning of friendship, love, and marriage. If you were to ask one-hundred people for their definitions, those words could likely mean something different to every single one of them.

The top three universal fundamentals in close relationships are transparency, vulnerability, and truth. You must truly live these principals to build and sustain lasting and meaningful relationships. Lisa and I have witnessed and chosen to live into these universal fundamentals that must be observed, felt, and lived in order to build and sustain a lasting life of friendship, love, and marriage.

Lisa was the first to offer transparency and vulnerability in our relationship. She chose to tell the 100% truth about the good, the bad, and the ugly of her life experiences up to the point of our meeting. She also took full responsibility for decisions where she knew that she could have made better choices or responded in a more ideal fashion regarding important life matters. Her authentic transparency and vulnerability are just two of her many amazing gifts.

When you surrender to vulnerability, you offer the opportunity for change and transformation. Lisa taught me how to surrender to my own vulnerability, which for me, took the form of removing my "superman cape." Before Lisa's help with my awakening, I didn't know what I didn't know regarding my superman cover. In order to ensure that my superman cover of mightiness was always present, I made sure that besides the cape that I was wearing, I had extras in the closet, trunk, office, and at our local dry cleaners.

While simple yet not easy, removing the superman cape and trashing all of my back-up capes gave me the power to surrender to vulnerability. My superman cape was originally worn by choice from the early days of growing up in the wonderful town of Hawthorne, Nevada. While I have a great sense of appreciation and respect for growing up in this unique environment, I had to deal with prejudice and an unlevelled playing field of real life.

Growing up with dark skin in a predominantly white town while immersed in a small ethnic neighborhood with a small-town population of 5,000 was very difficult. I was always reminded by "the powers that be" that I had to be at least twice as good in all of my efforts in order to possibly be judged on an equal scale with my white counterparts.

Rather than seeking to compete against others in an effort to get my needs met, I chose to see myself as my biggest competition. Whether I was engaged on the football field, at an art competition, or in the classroom, the other person was never my competition. I always chose to perform at the highest level seeking to improve my previous personal best, regardless of the discipline on which I was focused.

I saw the other people involved in any of the competitions as part of the game, not as someone to compete against! Being a person of color was simply my cross to bear this time around. I believe that we all have our own crosses to bear, and everyone is too *something* for someone else. You may be too tall, too short, too big, too smart, too weak, too dark, or too light for someone else. My guiding principle in matters like this is... Get over yourself and focus on striving to be your best regardless of who's on the playing field.

I chose to never take off my superman cape, believing the cape made everyone believe that I could do it all. I hoped that this would allow me a seat at the table. If my classmates and teachers believed that I could do it all well, maybe they wouldn't leave me out.

I figured out early on that my natural leadership skills had to continue growing in order to set me on a course to excel beyond all others. I had a faulty belief system at that time, and I mistakenly felt that I would be included if I was seen as a leader of my peers. This faulty thought system fueled my desire to lead. While I appreciate the desire to lead others, I'm happy to say that I have dropped my original juvenile reason for wanting to do so.

My chosen work ethic invested in over-serving and people-pleasing made me feel like I could outperform the masses in key areas of development. This became a seamless habit all the way through my seven years at the University of Nevada, Las Vegas. This superman complex became a subliminal part of my persona.

I extend enormous gratitude to Lisa for helping me permanently remove my superman cape. Now, I'm simply a human being, not a black man in white America trying to endlessly prove my value and worth in spite of my minority status. Lisa helped me get over myself! As we become more vulnerably human, we are able to have more authentic relationships with friends and loved ones. This in turn helps us build relationship equity and contributes immensely to how we leave others feeling.

Another influential "how we leave others feeling" highlight can be found in Lisa's story below about building relationship equity. Lisa recounts, "I was working in the television broadcasting industry at the UPN station in Las Vegas, Nevada, and was experiencing the onset of burn-out. I was a single mother with three children and zero ideas of what I could do beyond my broadcasting career.

The foundation of this career path began when I was sixteen years old. I didn't choose television broadcasting; it chose me based on my life's circumstances during that time.

Working in broadcasting finally took its toll, and I found myself wading in a dark and murky never-ending cesspool of drama. Have you ever felt totally misplaced or bewildered?

I was feeling broken, stuck, and very lost. A one-year rebound relationship failed miserably and left me feeling cheated and fractured. I was at an all-time low in my life and feeling like a failure in both my personal and professional life. I had suicidal thoughts. My three beautiful children kept me in this world.

I wanted to improve my ability to connect with others and elevate my public speaking skills. I joined toastmasters to help me practice the art of communicating more effectively and improve my public speaking skills.

It was through this organization that I learned of this personal and professional development vocation called life coaching. The thought of securing my very own life coach to help me figure things out from ground zero sounded very intriguing. I found Jesse through a referral from the general manager where I worked.

Up to this point, I had never held myself accountable in terms of personal growth and development. Not only was Jesse serving as my life coach, he was also my accountability partner, and he refused to let me off the hook when he knew I could be better and do better.

After doing "the work" and following my first 90-day plan review, I found that my ability to help people build their businesses could transfer over to coaching and helping people rebuild their lives. I then started building my exit strategy and professional bridge to leave my corporate broadcasting job.

Six months later, I opened my own coaching business, while still planning my corporate exit.

I was on track and had acquired six clients who I served before and after work hours. Then, the 2007 recession hit. This changed everything. As frustrating and draining as this was, I had to stay at the job where I was collecting a steady paycheck with medical benefits so that I could continue to provide a nice home and care for my children.

Another key reason for hiring my own life coach was to work through the process of finding a new job. My work environment became toxic when we hired a new senior account executive who I nicknamed "shark." She started going after my account list. After she snatched my third major account, I said *enough*! I couldn't take it anymore. And to make matters worse, her cubicle was right next to mine.

When she spoke, I found myself recoiling with disgust. I started resenting hearing the sound of her voice. I allowed her to get under my skin so badly. I felt hopeless. These dark and lonely feelings crowded every other thought in my mind. My biggest daily ritual was contemplating how and when to quit! I started doing more work away from the station to avoid her nonsense.

During my second session with Jesse, I shared this with him. He said, "Oh no, you are not quitting. When you go to your next job, there will be another Brandi." Jesse said my new strategy would be to stop building coping mechanisms and to build a winner's strategy. "You're going to transform her into feeling like you are best friends," he said.

My response to this was instantly combative and I said, "Like hell I am! That is never going to happen in a million years." He said the best way to tame a beast is to make them your best friend. Jesse said it is much harder to stab someone in the back if you are helping them feel better about their own being. He recommended that I start by asking her to lunch and use a "you-focused" approach to connecting with her.

This concept compels you to focus on the wants and needs of others first. This gets their attention and leaves them feeling like you care about them. Following a couple of "you-focused" lunch sessions with this former "mean girl," it broke the ice between us and we soon became best friends. She shifted from an attitude of dismissal regarding how she treated me to a matter of respect and care.

I would have never made this choice on my own. It truly created an amazing reversal of perspective, and my professional life stress was 100% removed regarding managing difficult coworkers. This would not have been possible without Jesse's amazing coaching recommendation to shift the relationship to a caring friendship. I was very authentic about growing my professional and personal relationships, and I found myself serving and caring about this woman's insecurities.

Fast forward fourteen years later, and we are still friends to this day. The best gift in this was that this choice allowed me to stop running from difficult people and to instead become creative about how to reverse my perspective by shifting the nature of the relationship. Speaking of this awesome new way of building relationship equity during the management of personal and professional life matters, I chose to take a closer look at my life choices.

Jesse and I built our amazing relationship from the foundation of friendship, which evolved while Jesse was coaching me. My ability to connect through the power of giving, thrusted Jesse and I into best-friend status quite quickly. Jesse is gentle in his teaching style. I really appreciated this about him. He made me feel that what I had to say mattered. As previously noted, our working relationship grew into a wonderful friendship. The more layers of my life that we peeled back together, and the more vulnerable I was in sharing them with him; the more a very special closeness grew. This was an intimacy that I had never felt with anyone else before.

This is where truth and transparency were born in our relationship. Do you have any idea how cool it is to be married to your best friend in the world? It is life changing on so many levels!

We were compelled to move into additional phases of our relationship beyond the coaching and friendship levels. Can you say intimacy on steroids? Because our coaching and friendship was so elevated, it brought the highest levels of love and physical intimacy to our relationship.

We had never been involved in a relationship with another person that brought so many jewels, insights, and room for continuous elevation before meeting one another! Our dedicated mannerisms set up massive support for an unbreakable relationship and pushed the concept of How You Leave Them Feeling to higher levels than we could ever imagine. Now, Jesse offers the power of our connection in the next passage."

Even though I had the fortune of building relationships with other women in my past, Lisa offered the mystery that was opposite from feeling like I had already been there and done that. Much like déjà vu, Lisa offered vu jàdé. The concept translates into doing something or experiencing something you are familiar with in a new way!

I was looking at all that I had previously experienced with a fresh set of eyes and no judgment! If you choose to take on the concept of vu jàdé regarding your important relationships, you will create terrific possibilities for all!

An additional benefit of practicing vu jàdé has been that it has made romantic connections extraordinary, and the exotic pull fostered new astronomical sexual relations. Our passion to connect with one another mentally, physically, emotionally, spiritually, intellectually, and erotically is astounding. Our desire to spend as much time together as possible is a testimony for the power of our connection and remains as a stimulant for our confidence and personal synergistic growth. We have also discovered that the more time that we spend apart from one another, the absence increases our desire and longing to reconnect as soon as possible.

We continue to be very mindful of the needs and desires of one another because we both know that whatever is going to happen in a long-term relationship has already happened...whether you remain open and aware to live and serve in the now will make the difference in your ultimate long-term future!

If you are looking to create an amazing life with your chosen partner, you must be focused and adopt a theme of Constant and Never-Ending Evolution to grow your power of presence. We call this living into the spirit of CANEE.

The concept of CANEE was built from a lifetime of striving to grow and develop while evolving along the way. So many of us give up or quit just before crossing the finish line. When you are running the race of life, tapping into the concept of CANEE says not only do you cross the finish line in record time, you may seek to run again and break your own previous record. The not-so-quiet hint here is to keep growing, keep getting better, and keep evolving.

Power of presence can be felt by those who have chosen to do the work to advance their emotional intelligence, social intelligence, and practical intelligence and remain in tune with how they are showing up. It also means being respectful of the choices that others make about their decision to show up...or not.

You can feel an attractive vibrational energy regarding someone who possesses a great power of presence. While owning confidence, charisma, and the ability to leave you feeling good about connecting with them, you can also sense at least a thread of vulnerability that makes them feel very real and approachable. Take a moment to pause from reading this chapter and think about how the concepts of friendship, love, and marriage leave you feeling.

Summary Points

Friendship, Love, and Marriage: Those Special Bonds

1. The fundamentals for growing your opportunities to harvest and live into friendship, love, and marriage start with three simple letters, TVT: transparency, vulnerability, and truth. Consider the value you will bring to your important relationships by offering transparency, vulnerability, and truth.

2. Just because you may have experienced countless other relationships, don't settle for déjà vu regarding your current one. Consider shifting to vu jàdé. Vu jàdé is experiencing something that you are already familiar with in a new way.

3. Being human and vulnerable can be one of the greatest tools for improving your friend and love relationships. If you're always wearing a superman cape, thinking you can do it all, and trying to prove yourself; your friends will not have the chance to get to know the real you.

Key Action Steps

Friendship, Love, and Marriage: Those Special Bonds

1. Think about your definitions of friendship, love, and marriage. Do they match those of your friends and loved ones? What do you need to do to close any gaps between the two?

2. Take a close look at the cover or covers (such as superman capes) you may be placing on yourself for the wrong reasons and choose to remove your covers in your quest for authenticity.

3. Always be willing to grow within your relationships. Know that this growth will be fueled by consistent dedication and focused work, referred to as Constant and Never-Ending Evolution (CANEE).

Chapter 9

Building Unbreakable Relationships

What is the value of building unbreakable relationships? The significance of building unbreakable relationships starts with the desire to make robust and sustainable connections within all of your relationships.

What is the predominant emotion you feel when you think of your significant other, business partner, family members, and friends? In order to connect with the best formula for success in building unbreakable relationships, you must be willing to get in touch with your real feelings.

This is the best time to practice developing your Emotional Intelligence (EI). We touched on this back in Chapter 3 as a building block to relationship equity, but it's also important to sustaining long-term relationships.

After years of focusing on our own personal development and witnessing the fluctuating emotions of countless coaching clients, Lisa and I can quickly identify people who are struggling to manage their emotions.

From our perspective, your EI refers to the ability to perceive, evaluate, and understand emotions. Knowing or learning how to use EI can positively help you relieve stress, communicate effectively, empathize with others, overcome challenges, and defuse conflict.

Using the power of EI elevates your communication and relationships. The more you are able to manage your emotions, the more you can meet others where they are so that your presence is always welcomed. When people you connect with feel you understand, care about, and appreciate them, the bond you build has the ingredients to become unbreakable.

The best path to fostering unbreakable relationships starts and ends by paying close attention to the concept of How You Leave Them Feeling. As you begin practicing leaving situations better than you found them and leaving others wanting more of your presence, you will be exhibiting character traits and behaviors that help you master the How You Leave Them Feeling concept.

As mentioned previously, the plight of all healthy human beings is that we are hardwired for survival. Those of us who are in the space of a strong positive mental attitude are focused on what it takes to survive. The four major needs that drive most of our concerns for survival are food, water, shelter, and sex.

If you refuse to eat food or drink water, you will not survive. If you don't choose to have the proper shelter for the environment that you live in, you will ultimately feel unsafe. If human beings refuse to have sex, we will die out as a species. If we don't pursue these four basic touchstones, our survival crumbles.

As we pursue the acquisition of food, water, shelter, and sex, we may appear to be driven by self-centered wants and needs. To build unbreakable relationships, we must do the emotional work it takes to grow beyond getting our own needs met. In other words, we have to get over ourselves and stop making our life quest all about us. As my good friend Dave Mann Sr. says, "Jesse, dude, why don't you get over your freaking self!"

When you are able to consistently demonstrate passion and care for the safety, well-being, and happiness of others, you ignite the opportunity to grow skyscraper structures in your relationships. People will be authentically drawn to you simply by your expression of How You Leave Them Feeling.

I have reconnected with people from my past, and then enjoyed those relationships for more than thirty years. Lisa and I recently participated in a virtual workshop where one of the participants told us that she only joined the workshop when she learned I was going to be the facilitator. Following the workshop, we received the following comment:

> "I met Jesse many years ago at the Riviera Hotel Casino in Las Vegas. I was his secretary for the last few months that he was serving as a Director of Player Development. He was very inspiring then too and just genuinely a good man with a lot of patience. I was fresh out of a farmtown in Illinois. This was my first job in Las Vegas. That incredibly brief relationship stuck with me all these years. Thank you for that!"

Before reading this takeaway from my former colleague, I had no idea how I had impacted the life of this single mother more than thirty years prior. I chose to support her development effort and provide an opportunity for her to do her best while growing her professional skillset. Even after reading her comments thirty years later, she still left me feeling inspired and astonished to know that my way of leading her professionally also impacted her personally. Now isn't this solid evidence of a truly unbreakable relationship?

Here's another example of an unbreakable relationship and how it developed. I met Charlie when I was the Director of Player Development at the Flamingo Hilton. He was one of our premium casino customers who played to the level of complimentary room, food, beverage, and first-class airfare.

Over the years and even after moving on to the Bellagio, I would make the time to call Charlie on a daily basis for a ten to fifteen-minute chat. I could feel his growing depression following the loss of his marriage and the abandonment by his four children. Even his close friends who knew him and his wife turned their backs on his friendship.

I truly didn't believe that I was making a big difference in his life, but my gut instinct (my intuition) said to stay in touch and make the calls. After a year of managing this routine with Charlie, I received an autographed photo and basketball of Michael Jordan. I was floored, so I called Charlie to ask him why he sent me such an amazing gift.

With tears in his eyes and shakiness in his voice he said, "For a full year, every time you called me—without knowing it—you talked the gun out of my mouth. I was contemplating taking my own life to relieve the grief, loss, disappointment, and feelings of failure."

For someone who feels very good about being able to speak in nearly any situation, I was completely speechless! My gut and intuition were connected to the reality of his vulnerability and the trusting of my intuition coupled with authenticity was music to his ears like a well-orchestrated symphony!

The takeaway? "It's good to be kind to everyone you meet...because everybody is battling something." Thinking about the depth and dynamics of my friendship with Charlie, I know that we will be friends for life. Unbreakable relationship! It's a great illustration of how your best and most sustainable relationships start and end with How You Leave Them Feeling.

If you are as moved as I continue to be regarding this friendship that began over twenty-three years ago, you are not alone. What were the real ingredients that built this unbreakable relationship? Kindness, empathy, care, consistency, awareness, intuition, love!

"The takeaway? 'It's good to be kind to everyone you meet... because everybody is battling something.'"

—Unknown

As you pursue the building or rebuilding of your relationships, consider incorporating these seven unbreakable relationship principles into all your interactions with others:

Kindness
Empathy
Care
Consistency
Awareness
Intuition
Love

The reasoning behind why these seven components lead to unbreakable relationships is as follows:

Kindness

Consistently delivering kindness to others not only offers the strong possibility of having kindness returned to you, but it also leaves you feeling good about bringing kind gestures to those who may be battling challenging matters. Your kindness is a welcomed gift to help lighten the load.

Empathy

When others receive empathy from you, it opens the door to proving that you have compassion for their particular circumstances. It offers a safe place for them to tell the truth about matters of concern.

Consistency

When you regularly make meaningful, positive infusions of what matters most to others, it leaves them feeling like they can constantly count on you to deliver.

Awareness

While many people are largely concerned with meeting their own needs, awareness gives us the ability to focus on the needs of others. This offers a sharp contrast to self-centeredness.

Intuition

When you are able to tap into the wants and needs of others through a feeling or instinct, that is using your intuition. Other people are generally appreciative to receive your outreach.

Love

We truly believe that sharing love with others is a universal concept. Love can be felt by others even when they aren't speaking the same language or when they come from a different origin. Sharing love with others reaches people at the heart and feeling level. Receiving an act of love leaves us feeling valued.

The seven unbreakable relationship principles we have developed are one of the reasons I believe our personal/professional development coaching business has gained so many loyal followers (or clients). That, combined with how we approach the "leave them wanting more" concept has resulted in a 97% approval rating.

This reveals itself in the fact that we have virtually never had a client quit. Whether we have spent one or 10 years together in a coaching relationship, our clients find closure by becoming so involved in their new way of life that they happily just evolve away from our services. It's an amazing testament to the success of the work.

Do any of your relationships need an injection of one or more these seven core principles?

Summary Points

Building Unbreakable Relationships

1. From our perspective, your EI refers to the ability to perceive, evaluate, and understand emotions. Learning to use EI positively can help you relieve stress, communicate effectively, empathize with others, overcome challenges, and defuse conflict. Using the power of EI elevates your communication and relationships, allowing you to meet others where they are and ensuring your presence is always welcome.

2. Basic human needs include food, water, shelter, and sex. We have to do the mental and emotional work it takes to go beyond those needs and consider other people's needs as well as our own. This contributes to building unbreakable relationships.

3. Applying the seven unbreakable relationship principles (kindness, empathy, care, consistency, awareness, intuition, love) to all your interactions with people are vital to building unbreakable relationships. Remember, we never know what other people are battling.

Key Action Steps

Building Unbreakable Relationships

1. Make a list of all your significant relationships and decide which ones are worthy of taking to the "unbreakable" level.

2. Review the list and determine which of your relationships need an injection of one or more

of the seven unbreakable relationship principles and start applying them now.

3. Read about emotional intelligence and see whether your behavior and attitudes are conducive to creating good relationship energy and equity in your life.

Chapter 10

Turning a Crisis Into Abundance

Have you ever found yourself at a crossroads when handling a challenging situation? Let's call these crossroads "experiences of managing catastrophic events." They can cause stress levels to rise. They often involve managing real-life losses and difficulties such as death of friends or family members, death of a child, fear of the unknown, unemployment, loneliness, depression, a downward change in health, managing blended families, or divorce. This chapter will offer you the opportunity to turn crises into abundance!

We've observed that people commonly think of stress as mainly a mental state of being. So many people stress out about things they only imagine, and this stress turns into FEAR. The best definition of this type of unnecessary stress-related FEAR is False Expectations Appearing Real!

Not only is this type of unnecessary stress-related fear a horrible experience, it effects more than just our minds. The Mayo Clinic has conducted studies proving that stress also produces a physical response.[10] Thousands of years ago, our fight-or-flight internal mechanisms kept us safe from predators. This stress kept us alive by flooding our bodies with cortisol and adrenaline to escape attacking animals or opposing tribes.

Today, our most stressful life events are much different. Oddly enough, our bodies still respond in the same way as primitive people did, which sometimes lead to illness. Richard S. Lazarus, American psychologist, professor, and researcher; is credited with creating the modern definition of stress. Richard's definition of stress involves the feelings we experience when "demands exceed the personal and social resources the individual is able to mobilize."

Stress can result from any of the major life events mentioned earlier, or even from a minor event like dropping a glass. Both of which can trigger a quick and decisive physical response (fight or flight).

In theory, once we remove the stressor, our bodies return to a neutral state. This perfect biological system is interrupted when we experience stressful life events that become chronic. A research team led by Carnegie Mellon University's Sheldon Cohen Doherty, Professor of Psychology within CMU's Dietrich College of Humanities and Social Sciences, has found that chronic psychological stress is associated with the body losing its ability to regulate the inflammatory response.[9]

This research also shows for the first time that the effects of psychological stress on the body's ability to regulate inflammation can promote the development and progression of disease. A state of heightened, chronic stress can lead to an increased risk of illness. Many inflammation-related illnesses can be very serious and life-threatening.

According to the American Psychological Association, chronic stress is linked to the six leading causes of death: heart disease, cancer, lung ailments, accidents, cirrhosis of the liver, and suicide. Why would you allow something as invasive and debilitating as stress put you at a high risk for death?

Part of keeping yourself healthy and able to attract and sustain healthy relationships is maintaining a healthy mind and point of view. That means not allowing your thoughts or unfortunate circumstances (such as the pandemic) to rule your mind and create stress while managing crossroads.

Whenever you find yourself at a crossroads, rather than focusing on the negative or the losses, you have an opportunity to manage the crisis and transform the situation. Ask yourself, which option will you choose?

When I met Lisa in October of 2005, she would come down with bronchitis as the year-end approached every single year. She was serving as an account executive selling television airtime, and the year-end expectations to meet quotas and goals brought on anxiety, fear, and loads of stress!

Management would revise budgets five and six times before coming to terms with one that would stick. Lisa worked 14 to 16 hours per day in order to hit her deadlines. This schedule would eventually cause chronic stress for weeks.

Those expectations coupled with her January sales performance expectations and the holiday demands created unimaginable stress. The additional stress of Christmas and gift-giving for friends, family, clients, colleagues, and bosses brought her unimaginable stress.

Moving into the New Year celebration after all that was too much for her. Her chronic stress progressed into an illness that would have her bedridden for weeks. Are you able to relate to this kind of cyclical stress that can bring you to your knees like Lisa?

Seek to change your thinking, regardless of whatever crossroads you are currently facing. Change your thinking...change your life! There are various ways to help you change your thinking. Your particular circumstances and personality will dictate the appropriate resources required to bring about change.

For example, if you're optimistic and motivated, and you like to read, you just might find the solution to your challenge in the next book you pick up. Which is exactly what happened to me when I found myself experiencing a professional life crisis. After working for more than thirty years with a degree in hotel administration from the University of Las Vegas, I found myself terminated from an executive marketing position. I truly couldn't believe that after all of the unpaid overtime, industry experience and superb colleague and client relationships, it just wasn't enough.

Rather than continuing to pursue a volatile career path with absolutely no value or measure for outstanding performance, I had to ask myself what would it take to avoid this situation in the future. The resolution came swiftly as I sought to find the answer to that one gigantic question: Why am I here on this earth—what is my purpose?

I picked up a book entitled *Action Strategies For Personal Achievement* by Brian Tracy, and it was a major home run! Although there are countless jewels in this book, the two golden nuggets that paved the path to discovering my purpose were as follows:

Nugget #1
I learned that my purpose was wrapped in my best gifts and talents; that's what I was born to give to this world. If you do not know your best gifts and talents, ask 10–15 people who know you well. The people that I asked unanimously said that my gifts were found in guiding, directing, and leading others. Can you say "wow"? I had no idea until those fifteen people pointed that out.

Nugget #2
Brian Tracy said that if you choose to read an hour a day in your field of study, you could become an expert

in that field in five years. I can't speak about where Mr. Tracy found evidence to support his statement, but I trusted him. It gave me great joy to know that I could shift from a long career in hospitality to a new vocation in personal and professional development as a success coach and inspirational speaker.

Again, Tracy's book was the catalyst that helped me change my thinking from being stuck in a dead-end hospitality career to thriving in a limitless vocation in the personal and professional development field.

While this is a great example of how one book sparked the flame in one person, your story may be different. It may take a different type of resource to ignite a positive change in you. The moral of this story is to seek additional resources beyond your own mind to help you change your thinking in order to bring about positive change.

Rather than overcomplicating how we can create a positive turnaround in the mix of professional challenges, Lisa and I have elected to invoke Ockham's Razor concept that we introduced in Chapter 1. Ockham's Razor is easily paraphrased by saying, "the simplest explanation is most likely the right one." It is a problem-solving principle that brings much promise to the plethora of concerns we are all faced with solving daily. This is closely related to picking up a single book that may guide and direct you to a positive solution for complicated problems.

In alignment with Ockham's Razor, we created and live into our AAA Life Strategy Concept for sailing through rough waters during stormy seasons like the one we are currently navigating: a global pandemic. Consider embracing our AAA Life Strategy Concept to create a turnaround in your world.

AAA Life Strategy Concept

Our AAA Life Strategy Concept was born in this era of overcoming life challenges.

It's a simple concept that propels us into a position to thrive, not just survive, during the impact of managing the unknown in the face of a serious global negative impact!

The first A in this life strategy concept stands for Attitude. Take a close look at your attitude and determine what your ongoing disposition is relative to how you feel about the difficulties and unknown effects this global crisis is having on you and those you love and care about.

Surround yourself with trusted advisors and people who can help you tell the truth about your attitude, while strategically looking to either maintain or return to a good place of being.

Your attitude is what either attracts or repels people. They either want to be connected with you or want to run for the hills to get away from your negative attitude. If you have a glowing and attractive attitude, people will appreciate you, as it is not a very common trait. Use your attractive glow to connect with and infuse your positive energy and vibration into the lives of others.

While a caustic, negative attitude destroys you from the inside out, it will also instill negative emotions in those you touch. As human beings, we are "like for like" creatures. Your positive attitude may truly be the difference maker in the lives of many!

The second powerful A in our life strategy concept is Adjust. Don't settle for merely surviving difficult things. Be very clear on what adjustments you need to make to position yourself to thrive, even when the world seems to be falling apart.

You might say this is easier said than done, but what we say is...if not said, likely not done! Consider using your best creativity to connect with other positive people to help you create a pleasing life by any positive means necessary. Be sure you make any adjustments necessary to sustain a pleasing attitude.

The final powerful A in our life strategy concept is Adapt. Make sure you are willing and able to adapt a forward-thinking life strategy that brings together a consistently positive attitude following your prudent adjustments. Choose to continue rising again...again, and again!

Live by the expression, "You are either up or getting up!" Whenever you find yourself slipping down a pattern of darkness and it feels like life is getting the best of you, use our AAA life strategy to simplify whatever you feel is complex. Adhering to our AAA Life Strategy Concept can create a positive turnaround in the right direction!

Not Starting All Over

Another concept we use when coaching individuals is what we call "Starting over, not starting all over again." This can provide a new way to view problems and potentially transform a crisis into a more manageable situation.

Lisa explains how this helped her: "The magic of 'starting again' felt so much lighter than starting **ALL** over again during a period in my life when things were very uncertain. I learned the subtle yet powerful difference after spending one week in Salt Lake City, Utah with my sister, Leslie. We teamed up for purging and packing up the apartment where my mother had lived for more than fifteen years. We were all exhausted.

After returning home, I woke up the next morning and felt like I was dying. I was pushed to my wits end mentally, emotionally, spiritually, and physically. I went from feeling like a hero to feeling like a zero overnight. How did this happen in the blink of an eye?

I thought to myself, I have just quit my career with a six-figure salary, and I didn't have a clue how or why it all happened. I felt my personal and professional signature was tied into my existence and being. Without my corporate career, I felt like a nobody. Broadcasting was all that I had known since I was sixteen years old. What was I going to do now that I am retired—die? I felt like I was stuck on the negative side of the old GRASP concept, which stands for Getting Ready, Attitude, Signature, and Passion.

Jesse and I created a new version of the traditional concept that serves to keep people stuck in their failing attitudes and behaviors. Our new GRASP concept encourages people to reverse the perspective of what we have all been taught. This reversal starts with the letter in the middle: the letter A is the key to change and transformation. It represents taking a fresh look at your attitude with the opportunity to shift the perspective from commonplace to extraordinary, and the opportunity to live the life you design.

Your signature, or personal branding of how others have come to know you, is the next element to increase the quality of how you do things. The final step is exhibiting a passion that tells the world that you love what you are doing and you are crystal clear in why you are doing it!

I had to find a way to fully embrace and live into our new GRASP concept following the exit from my career in January 2013. I didn't have a clue how I would find joy and happiness in my new life as a retiree. I found myself seemingly dependent on eight different medications, all prescribed by my doctor whom I knew, liked, and trusted. At the height of my anxiety, I was taking 20 milligrams of Lexapro, 10 milligrams of Zolpidem (sleeping pills), a muscle relaxer, 1800 milligrams of Motrin, hydrocodone pain pills, and birth control.

I woke up feeling like a zombie every morning. I couldn't laugh, cry, feel, or even think for myself. I was very scared, lost, and lonely. At this moment in time, I knew that I should be feeling joyful, excited, and full of life and love. I had just moved into a gorgeous home with the man of my dreams, Jesse.

Yet, I felt scared and more insecure than I had ever felt in my life. My medications were stealing all of my thoughts and feelings. My brain wasn't firing right, and I often couldn't speak intelligently, if at all.

I researched a new doctor for my quest for better help and health beyond medications. I wanted a caring doctor who wouldn't simply prescribe more meds and who would understand and listen to my wishes to get off ALL of the above-mentioned medications. I knew it could be dangerous to stop medicines suddenly without consulting a doctor.

I asked this new doctor to please help me with a weaning schedule. He wrote out my weaning schedule on a yellow Post-it note. It spanned four weeks. When I got to day three and felt worse than ever before, I knew that the weaning schedule was too aggressive. I was having withdrawals, shaking, and wanted to vomit. I felt like I had a bad flu.

I told Jesse how horrible I was feeling and how scared I was. I showed him the four-week schedule that the doctor had given me, and Jesse said, 'I'm no doctor, but this is way too aggressive.'

Jesse and I worked together along with medical professionals to create a realistic weaning schedule. I then called my dear friend, Paul Grady, who was a nutritional scientist. I shared my story above with him and asked for his help. He had me fill out a health survey to check my symptoms. He prescribed a weekly regimen of several vitamins.

I took the prescribed vitamins three times a day for twelve weeks. I would diligently document how I was feeling morning, noon, and night and check in with Jesse and Paul to ensure that I was on the right track. The results were nothing short of a miracle. After the twelve weeks, I felt alive and better than my original, normal self!

Following this positive progression, it was magical to one day wake up and be able to feel, think, and appreciate vivid colors in the sky and the beauty of nature once again. I felt like I was alive, whereas before, I felt like an invalid—listless and desperately wanting to die. And these results were achieved by simply changing my perspective from starting ALL over again to starting again. Starting all over again felt like an undoable challenge. Starting again reminded me to bring the best gifts and talents I had built throughout my professional career.

Now, it was time to start living into my new vocation and partnership with JessTalk Speaking & Coaching Firm. Jesse put together a sales competition to see who would get the most sales in a month. He did this with the most heartfelt of intentions. With twenty-four years of sales experience and a competitive nature, this would get me motivated and ready to hit the ground running.

However, I told him that wasn't a fair playing field, considering he had been running the company for ten years. I couldn't compete with his existing relationship database. 'You can pick up the phone and ask any of your clients to fill an event, give you a referral, or purchase our latest offering.' While the sales competition wasn't particularly alluring, the process of designing my new life path and bringing all my jewels and nuggets of wisdom to the table was exhilarating!

I was ready to put down all of what no longer served me and create a life of the things that I loved to do and things that I was very good at… **BY DESIGN!**

When I joined JessTalk Speaking & Coaching Firm, Jesse already had a business plan. We simply needed to incorporate areas where I could contribute based on my previous experience. Upon review of his recommendations, I was surprisingly overwhelmed.

My mind wasn't in any shape to be dealing with things like this. We took a drive, and he asked me if I had reviewed the updated plan. I panicked and felt like I was choking and suffocating. I felt an enormous amount of pressure to perform when I couldn't. I couldn't even think straight. Jesse said, 'What is it that is written in this business plan that is making you feel this way?'

I said I wasn't sure. It just didn't feel right to me. Jesse said, 'Okay, let's tear up these pages and start over with a blank sheet of paper. You can write down the things that you enjoy and like to do and only do those things. I will continue to do everything else.'

I felt such a relief in Jesse saying these words. I started with reviewing our existing contracts and rates. I immediately tripled our rates and exponentially grew our revenue after the first year. I also created and managed a Facebook business page. I put together marketing sheets for the company and for each of Jesse's keynotes. I also put together proposals that were not just one-and-done.

We would now have offerings to present after a corporate coaching keynote, workshop, or training session so the participants could implement what they had just learned. Typically, when participants leave, they stay enthusiastic for a day or two, and then the momentum wears off. To get sustainable and long-lasting results, it takes a twelve-month commitment with a maintenance plan to ensure what we've taught sticks. Without accountability, the client and the team are off the hook. We have gained long-term, sustainable clients using this strategy.

This was the perfect way for me to put the skills I had developed to work for my new endeavor. It was truly a practice of 'starting over, not starting all over again,' and was an effective method for dealing with my need to transform a personal crisis. It also represented the new GRASP concept in action. I shifted my perspective from commonplace to extraordinary…and started living my life by design."

Reversal of Perspective

Choosing to "start over" rather than "start all over again" is based on a simple reversal of perspective. Lisa says: "For the thirty-five years that I worked in corporate America, I was surrounded by professionals who boasted about their college degrees. Not having a college degree to hang on my wall to indicate to others that I was just as intelligent as they were left me feeling devastated.

During those early years, many of the jobs I applied for required a college degree. This prerequisite intimidated me, and I always felt insecure and less qualified than those who hung fancy pieces of paper on their walls with a host of titles and initials following their name.

Anytime I walked into an interview, I was very nervous about them asking me why I didn't go to college and get a degree. Fortunately, my talents and gift of gab carried the interviews, and the question never came up.

When I got my first job, I loved it. It was sexy working at a television station. I met many celebrities coming in and out of the station. This was about 1981 when Microsoft Word was just being released as the newest and greatest technology. This was going to take over the typewriter with word processing and be so much more efficient. I loved my job and felt very empowered. I went to the community college to take classes for word processing. While this was helpful, it wasn't enough to earn me the honor of hanging that fancy piece of paper on the wall.

Fast forward to January 2013. Jesse and I were having a conversation about going to college. He has two college degrees. I was sharing with him how inferior I felt that I didn't go to college and get a degree. Jesse said, 'Do you know that just because someone goes to college and gets a degree doesn't mean that they are smarter than you?' Then he said, 'Wait a minute. Do you realize how many hours of life training you have pursued for the last thirty-two years? You have endured two divorces, managed several high-powered jobs, been responsible for raising three amazing children, and have done it pretty much single-handedly.' Jesse calculated over 300,000 hours that I had spent learning how to raise my children while managing to stay gainfully employed.

On January 18, 2013, Jesse presented me with my own PhD framed certificate of achievement. It was from Las Vegas Life University with the certification of Life Major and People Minor. Jesse said this PhD degree stands for Personal Happiness Decision.

Jesse said, 'You chose to invest your energy, intelligence, and resources into raising healthy children. This is a MAJOR accomplishment, and it's time you start living the appreciation of such an endeavor, regardless of the name of the university and initials behind the names. Your PhD is second to none!'

Finally, Jesse said, 'Graduating from the school of hard knocks along with the countless hours you have put in learning how to be street smart versus book smart is certainly a worthy accomplishment, and you must stand proud representing to the world that you truly are good enough!'

His words and actions were a game changer! This was a major reversal of perspective, and I know that not many people who have felt the way I did in the past can walk away feeling as great and successful as I currently feel.

Through my important conversations with Jesse, I can chalk this up to another stage of starting again versus feeling like I have to start all over again to be equal in talents to others. Jesse helped me rethink what I had already achieved and start my thinking again from that point. This was a real 'wow' moment!

See a copy of my PhD on the following page."

As a result of reading about these key life-changing moments, can you feel how important it is to be aware of your self-talk and the choice of words that you use? Something as simple as telling yourself that you're starting again, versus telling yourself that you're starting ALL OVER again, is empowering. It goes to prove that living your life by design can be positively impacted by the words that you use and the thoughts you think. As previously mentioned...Change your thinking... Change your life!

Although the title of this book is *How You Leave Them Feeling* with the subtitle of *The Foundation for Inspiring Love & Relationships*, it's also about how you leave yourself feeling!

When I helped Lisa change her point of view and shift her negative self-talk, she was able to focus on her major accomplishments that didn't come with a degree. This is an important illustration of how changing your perspective can change your life.

Where in your life is it necessary for you to change your perspective and eliminate debilitating thoughts about yourself so you can live your best life?

We trust this chapter offered you a nugget or two that you will use to turn your crisis situations into abundance versus living a defeated and unenthusiastic lifestyle when you are faced with repetitive negative thoughts and difficult problems to solve.

Summary Points

Turning a Crisis Into Abundance

1. To transform a crisis, we must find ways to reduce and eliminate fear and stress. Stress is a physical response in our body to a perceived threat and

this causes us to feel fearful and anxious. Often, stress is a result of "false expectations appearing real." We can learn to change our thinking so that we do not conjure up reasons to be stressed unnecessarily.

2. Use the AAA Life Concept Strategy to productively move through a crisis. It starts with examining your **attitude** about the crisis and determining whether you can see it from a different perspective. Be very clear on how you need to **adjust** in order for you to position yourself to thrive. Finally, make sure you are willing and able to **adapt** a positive, forward-thinking life strategy.

3. When you find yourself carrying around negative thoughts about your past life choices and feeling like you have to start all over again, be willing to reverse your perspective to one of "starting again" rather than "starting all over again." Words and thoughts are powerful and can dramatically change how you see and resolve harmful or destructive situations. Shift your words to move through the crisis, seek to keep only the lesson from a problem, and create a strategy for using those lessons to create abundance.

Key Action Steps

Turning a Crisis Into Abundance

1. Make a detailed list of the pros and cons related to the crisis. List and rate the essential facts of concern for each company. Use a 10-point scale, whereby 1 represents a shallow perceivable value, and 10 represents the highest value.

Calculate the total of your ratings of all of your facts of concern.

A sample rating system between Century 21 or Keller Williams brokers is on the following page.

Century 21 has a total of 7.3 on a 10-point scale, and Keller Williams Realty has a capacity of 5.2 on the same 10-point scale. This comparison represents a 2-point favor for Century 21. Using this Crisis Management Pros & Cons tool can help lend weight to making a prudent choice of real estate brokers.

PROBLEM TO SOLVE—DO I CHANGE REAL ESTATE BROKERS?
CRISIS MANAGEMENT PROS & CONS RATING SCALE

Facts of Concern	Century 21 Pros & Cons	Facts of Concern	Keller Williams Realty Pros & Cons	Point Variance
1	7	Downtown location	4	Keller Williams Realty Location	−3
2	9	Luxury listing value	5	Luxury listing value	−4
3	6	Commissions	9	Commissions	3
4	8	Fees	6	Fees	−2
5	7	Leads	4	Leads	−3
6	7	Marketing expenses	3	Marketing expenses	−4
7	8	Transition factor	5	Transition factor	−3
8	8	Broker quality	7	Broker quality	−1
9	8	Development opportunity	5	Development opportunity	−3
10	6	Autonomy	8	Autonomy	2
11	9	Signing bonus	0	Signing bonus	−9
12	8	Access to key personnel	9	Access to key personnel	1
13	9	Benefits package (referrals agent)	4	Benefits package (referrals agent)	−5
14	7	Compensation package	5	Compensation package	−2
15	8	Customer factor (quality and quantity of customers)	6	Customer factor (quality and quantity of customers)	−2
16	4	Professional expectations	6	Professional expectations	2
17	5	Freedom factor—freedom for getting job done	8	Freedom factor—freedom for getting job done	3
18	9	Future longevity (how long can it remain like this)	6	Future longevity (how long can it remain like this)	−3
19	8	Lifestyle affected	4	Lifestyle affected	−4
20	7	Their management style	7	Their management style	0
21	7	Reputation, integrity and delivering as promised	5	Reputation, integrity and delivering as promised	−2
22	6	Stress level and pressure	6	Stress level and pressure	0
23	5	Team fair play occupational hazard and people Factor	4	Team fair play occupational hazard and people factor	−1
24	8	Work environment and company culture	5	Work environment and company culture	−3

7.3		5.2	

Century 21	Keller Williams Realty	Total Point Variance
7.3	**5.2**	**2.01**

Crisis Management Pros & Cons Rating Scale
0 = very low perceivable value
10 = highest perceivable value

PROS & CONS SIMPLE VIEW

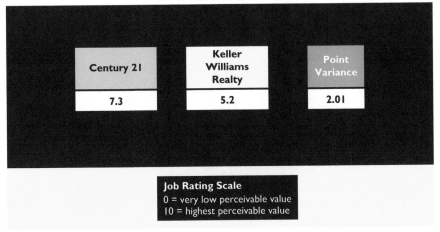

Century 21	Keller Williams Realty	Point Variance
7.3	5.2	2.01

Job Rating Scale
0 = very low perceivable value
10 = highest perceivable value

2. Apply our AAA Life Strategy to the crisis you are facing. Examine your attitude about it, adjust your view of it, and adopt a positive forward-thinking focus.

3. Remember that resolving a crisis does not necessarily require you to start from the beginning. Learn to appreciate the experiences and skills you have acquired in life and apply them in a new way through a "reversal of perspective."

Chapter 11

Work and Love—It's All in the Balance

We have encountered many dedicated professionals who have a hard time balancing the number of hours they dedicate to their professional and personal relationships. While those relationships are intertwined at various points, you will find great value in learning to manage these two pillars separately and with mutual respect.

Masses of people worked from home both during and after the Covid-19 pandemic. Working from home can either be very challenging, or it can be a great opportunity.

At the beginning of the pandemic, many employees struggled to adapt to online tools. They also struggled to fulfill their professional responsibilities in their personal spaces. However, within a short period of time, people managed to develop the necessary tools for working digitally. Whenever possible, many workers started using collaboration platforms and video conferencing to engage and get their work done.

While some people enjoyed being able to eliminate travel time when working remotely from home, several drawbacks were also identified; such as the lack of face-to-face discussion and in-person informal meetings.

Whether you are commuting to work or working remotely, time is your most valuable commodity. We respect the commodity of time and live by the model of "time and timing." The model of time and timing means that you maintain complete respect for how you choose to use your time at work and in your personal life.

When you engage others in personal or professional collaborations, ensure that the timing is right for all parties. Don't assume that just because you feel it is crucial and the timing is right for you that it is also suitable for others.

With this concept, you must consider the resources you devote to your personal life, professional growth, and success. Ensure that you have consistent strategic conversations with yourself and significant others about managing personal and professional pillars to bring the healthiest balance to you and your relationships.

When it comes to holding respect for the "time and timing" concept, we use one of our business rules to help govern our time. Our business operating hours are from 6 a.m. to 6 p.m. Outside of those hours, we put our work down.

We shut down all business conversations and client matters at 6 p.m. every day. We do this in order to make the shift from our work life to our personal life. The only interruption we allow is when a client calls with an emergency.

Whenever we accept an emergency client call after 6 p.m., we must take the call away from our home and work zone. It must be taken outside in order to preserve the energy and vibration of the space that we call home. Respecting this business rule allows the other partner to simply live and not feel stuck in high-pressure work mode endlessly. We both love and respect this business rule as it allows controllable matters to be managed efficiently and respectfully to all.

Even if you aren't choosing to design business rules to help you manage work and life, know this: work and love—it's all in the balance. You heard it more than once by now, "It's All About How You Leave Them

"It's All About How You Leave Them Feeling!"

—Jesse Ferrell

Feeling!" This also includes how you leave yourself feeling. Consider the following guiding principles related to work that will afford you the opportunity to embrace a road map for success while leaving yourself and others feeling great.

Guiding Principles for Work and Relationships

1. Determine your most productive hours for excelling in your professional space.
2. Take periodic breaks for at least five minutes following an hour of full concentration.
3. Determine a work schedule that allows you to serve with full commitment.
4. After completing your work commitment, put down all professional concerns.
5. Build love, creativity, and organic sharing within your important relationships.

As we break down these foundational guiding principles, remain open to how they can help you manage the coordination between your work and personal life.

#1 Determine your most productive hours for excelling in your professional space

Simply clocking in at the required time during your work hours is only part of your commitment. Various studies have shown that the average worker is productive for only three hours per day. You may be asking what in the world are workers doing with the other five hours during a full eight-hour workday? Great question, and I believe there are countless answers.

We highly recommend that you push to be very intentional during your workday. A great start to ensuring you establish respectful intentions about what you want to accomplish during the workday is to look at your commitments and work plans the night before. Set intentions the night before for maximum productivity during the workday.

When you start your workday, take one more look at the intentions for productivity that you highlighted the evening before. Once you press the green light to start your day, stay focused on moving through commitments efficiently. Don't allow energy thieves to rob you of your time, productivity, and intentions.

An energy thief is someone who exhausts time with meaningless conversation like gossip. We recommend that you place energy thieves in your nonnegotiable bucket. Sometimes that can be very difficult if the energy thief is persuasive or connected in some way that leaves you feeling obligated. You may encounter energy thieves that show up as coworkers, friends of coworkers, bosses, or people from other departments who have a certain level of status that must be respected.

We have a strategy that has worked well for the clients we have served over the years who find themselves in predicaments with energy thieves. This is our Variable Exit Strategy.

Variable Exit Strategy—Slow, Medium, and Fast

When you are being pulled in by an energy thief, use one of the following strategies to escape:

Slow Exit Strategy

If there is an important person who has introduced you to someone who turns out to be an energy thief, you must exit slowly and gracefully. You'll invest more time with this person than you truly want to because you are respecting the important person that introduced you, and you don't want to embarrass your key contact.

If it turns out that your key contact learned that you didn't stay the course for the entire time because you exited slowly, you can share with them that you gave sufficient respect and time to the energy thief and feel good about it.

Medium Exit Strategy

When you are sharing space with an energy thief who isn't a direct connection, you may exit after investing a medium amount of time. In other words, you don't have to make it a slow exit, costing you precious time. The modest amount of time that you choose to offer in situations like this will be enough to justify a respectful offering of your time in the company of someone who was stealing your energy.

Fast Exit Strategy

Whenever you find yourself in the space of an energy thief and there is no formal connection, just simply run for the hills as quickly as you can. Spare yourself the pain of being in the presence of someone who is robbing you of inner peace and precious time! You don't owe anyone anything at all, and you have the right to regain your time.

Now that you are equipped with a strategy to recover your best time and timing, let's take a look at other challenges with work-life balance. You may encounter other workers who constantly interrupt your flow with nonprofessional matters. It's highly acceptable to take occasional breaks from your focus to connect with coworkers for brief informal conversations; however, the key word here is brief. If you choose to add more bandwidth to building relationship equity with others, be mindful that it's best to schedule time for longer detailed conversations before or after your workday.

You will be very pleased with your production levels when you set powerful intentions by managing the nature of your communication with others. We're familiar with the phrase, "Time flies when you are having fun." It's an added bonus to be in a position where you may have a little fun during the workday. However; if not managed, time can get away from you, and it's impossible to recover lost time!

#2 Take periodic breaks for at least five minutes following an hour of full concentration

You will have more energy at the end of a workday whenever you are able to consistently take a five-minute break after dedicated concentration. If our occupation doesn't allow for periodic breaks, or if someone else governs your breaks, ensure you take advantage of their best offering. If someone else governs your breaks differently, ensure to take advantage of their best offering.

#3 Determine a work schedule that allows you to serve with full commitment

While we all have different levels of concentration, you must find your place in a zone that serves how you best work and what is best for those you are serving. Never give up on finding harmony between how you like to work and what is expected of you.

#4 After completing your work commitment, put down all professional concerns

Depending on the type of work or service you provide, it can be very difficult to put down your workday when the demand for your work or services is continuous. Whenever you encounter circumstances where the demand is greater than the supply, your best opportunity to maintain good health is to set the appropriate boundaries, allowing you to stop work and move into your personal time.

#5 Build creativity and organic sharing with your important relationships

Your important relationships are best served by adding creative touches to them. Throw out the cookie-cutter style of doing the same things with the same people all the time. Periodically offer surprising new activities that bring joy to you and others as you continue to develop your important relationships. A time-tested relationship enhancer happens whenever you engage in interesting conversation.

It is a huge gift to love your work. It's an even greater gift whenever you learn how to balance the love of your work and other important life matters.

Summary Points

Work and Love—It's All in the Balance

1. Regardless of how hard you work, be mindful that there is life before, during, and after work. While you are seeking to serve others in your professional and personal life, always remember that how you leave yourself feeling is important.

2. Balancing work and life have become even more important since the work environment was transformed by the Covid-19 global pandemic. Defining your work style and structuring your workday are important to your own self-care and to the relationships you have with others.

3. Five practical guidelines for work and relationships include identifying your productive hours, taking breaks during the day, creating a feasible work schedule, letting your work go when it is

completed, and bringing creativity into your important relationships.

Key Action Steps

Work and Love—It's All in the Balance

1. Have consistent strategic conversations with yourself and significant others about how to manage both your personal and professional life in a way that brings the healthiest balance for self, your family, and your professional associations.

2. Consider designing "Business Rules" to help you define how you want to manage your business life and protect your personal life.

3. Practice the five guiding principles for work and relationships so that you have the opportunity to embrace a road map for success while leaving yourself and others feeling great.

Chapter 12

Conclusion: How Do You Leave People Feeling?

We encourage you to put these principles into practice and answer one major question: How Do You Leave People Feeling?

We trust that you have found nuggets of value throughout this book. We are living in unique times where there is so much uncertainty about the quality of our health and lives. There are countless people who are suffering and who are hungry for positive, meaningful relationships.

We teamed up to write this book in an effort to provide you with proven and tested practices on how to attract and grow the most meaningful relationships. When you surround yourself with positive, inspirational people, you will gain the opportunity to live an enriched life. Building meaningful quality relationships pushes the envelope on living a life of joy.

How You Leave Them Feeling: Your Foundation for Inspiring Love & Relationships is a very important foundational concept. It allows you to gain value in your life by simply leaving everyone you meet and everything you touch better than you found them. All you have to do is think about the concept, and you will already be on your way to greatness!

A few of our favorite principles are as follows:

The Umuntu Factor
Turning a Crisis Into Abundance
Living Life by Design

The Umuntu Factor

"Umuntu ngumuntu ngabantu." Umuntu is translated to mean, "I am, because you are." The entire Zulu tribe phrase, "Umuntu ngumuntu ngabantu" literally means that a person is a person through other people.

We need one another. We are able to continue growing and evolving because of our relationships. Together we can build schools, homes, communities, cities, provinces, countries and...lives! The Umuntu Factor is alive and well... Whose lives will you touch now?

Turning a Crisis Into Abundance

Seek to change your thinking, regardless of whatever crossroad you are currently facing. Change your thinking...Change your life!

Remember that resolving a crisis does not necessarily require you starting from the beginning. Learn to appreciate the experiences and skills you have acquired in life and apply them in a new way through a "reversal of perspective."

Living Life by Design

Living life by design means that you take the time to develop and create the important areas of your life. Living life by happenstance occurs without your awareness. Living your life by design happens when you refuse to just stand by and wait to see what life may or may not bring you.

We trust our book inspires you to start living your life by design rather than happenstance!

We ask that you immediately start applying your favorite principles, recommendations, or lessons that you have learned from our real-life case studies featured in this book.

You have left us both feeling honored and appreciated for investing your precious time and resources to read this book in hopes that you will discover useful and sustainable value!

You can find other helpful information on our website. Please go to the following website for additional information: www.jesstalk.com

Hire us for:

Leadership Development & Motivational Speaking

Our speaking style focuses on your highest wants and needs for a highly customized workshop, keynote, and training program.

https://jesstalk.com/solutions/solutions-for-business/speaking/

Hire us for:

Personal or Professional Success Coaching

We help you create an incentive towards your DESIRED growth and development. We aim to deliver measurable outcomes through our **DESIRE** process.

Here is the **DESIRE** breakdown:

Discovery – Engage – Strategy – Implement – Results – Evaluate

https://jesstalk.com/solutions/solutions-for-you/personal-success-coaching/

Hire us for:

The Breakthrough Success Plan – 9-Week Online Course

The Breakthrough Success Plan is a Signature Branding, Leadership Development, and Opportunity Creation system designed for the growth of business professionals.

These three key success pillars will gain you the **recognition** you deserve, the income that you want, and a life of **fulfillment** beyond your imagination.

https://www.thebreakthroughsuccessplan.com

About the Authors

Lisa Ferrell

Lisa Ferrell is a JessTalk Speaking & Coaching Firm partner, master success coach, and strategist. She also runs LisaListen, a JessTalk Speaking & Coaching Firm division that primarily focuses on helping women around the globe improve the quality of their lives! She has thirty-five years of broadcast television, radio, and outdoor sales and marketing advertising experience.

She spent a fair share of her corporate career as a media buyer and sales planner for several national advertising agencies. Lisa obtained her coaching certification from Coach U in 2006 in San Diego, California, and has been inspiring and leading others since she graduated. Clients have come to appreciate her unique style of direct, to-the-point delivery. Lisa has a keen focus on helping her clients get the results they want in life.

As an expert in helping others, Lisa pulls together the critical parts of sales and marketing that will ensure women get noticed. She helps clients discover their core values, identify their goals, and assist with behavior change, resources, and education to help them attain the vision they desire for their lives.

Jesse Ferrell

Jesse attended the University of Nevada, Las Vegas, on multiple academic scholarships, where he earned degrees in fine arts and hotel administration. He spent six years as an adjunct professor teaching senior-level casino marketing classes at the University of Nevada, Las Vegas. He worked in the hospitality and gaming industry for thirty-six years, starting as a bus boy and moving to the highest management levels as the casino marketing executive director.

Jesse earned his coaching certification in 2007 from Coach U in Chicago, Illinois. This one endeavor enabled him to live out his purpose and passion, using his gifts and talents to educate and inspire others to live into their highest vision.

Since the inception of JessTalk Speaking & Coaching Firm in 2001, Jesse has served top executives and professionals in the entertainment industry, including many that have risen through multiple senior-level positions since they enrolled in JessTalk. He takes great pleasure in creating partnerships with professionals and facilitating communication and leadership development workshops with them and their teams.

JessTalk Speaking & Coaching Firm has found enormous life-changing value in serving clients such as Decode Digital Marketing & Advertising, Robert Lee & Associates, Sierra Nevada Corporation, Apple Computers, MGM Resorts International, Encore & Wynn Las Vegas, Canada Scaffold, University of Nevada Las Vegas, Liberty Tax, US Ecology, Real Time Networks, and countless domestic and international businesses.

Over three decades, Jesse has developed connections with a wide range of personalities and professionals from actors and tennis players to world-champion bull riders; such as Whoopie Goldberg, Bruce Willis, Muhammad Ali, Zina Garrison, and Charles Sampson to name a few.

Other creative endeavors include JessTalk Radio, hosted by Jesse and Lisa; Conversations, a podcast featuring a broad range of talents partaking in spontaneous conversation; and Brothers & Conversations, a podcast created with Shaundell Newsome, founder and visionary for

Sumnu Marketing. All of which are available at one of the following: JessTalk.com (media section), iTunes, Facebook, Apple Podcasts, Spotify, Stitcher, or YouTube.

How You Leave Them Feeling: Your Ultimate Key to Personal & Professional Success was the first book authored by Jesse in 2006. Louis Gossett Jr. wrote the foreword and Brian Tracy, the celebrity speaker and author who was a devoted mentor to Jesse, wrote a testimonial for his book. Tracy is the man responsible for piquing Jesse's interest in speaking and coaching as a vocational choice more than twenty-two years ago. The second edition of *How You Leave Them Feeling: Your Ultimate Key to Personal & Professional Success* was published in 2022.

Other Works by the Authors

Jesse chose to write this inspirational book for anyone who wants to live a happier and more fulfilled life. He shares that the How You Leave Them Feeling concept can be incorporated into your everyday life to achieve immediate, effective, and rewarding results.

The goal of this book is to innovate your quality of life by allowing a diverse and broad range of associations, cultures, and humanities influence your thoughts and perspectives.

COMING SOON!

Content Readers

The quality of this book would not be possible without the support, time, and attention invested by our amazing content readers. Around the globe, we are all living busy and productive lives during extremely challenging times.

Our content readers were asked to read the first three chapters of our coauthored book. We have taken into consideration all of their helpful recommendations for improvement.

We have immense gratitude and appreciation for Caren Becker, Christina Ciccone, Devin Hyden, Ernie Becker, Jenni Murphy, Julie Neil, Lisa Czjaka, Lisa Ulshafer, Pat Mclellan, Robert Ciccone, and Wendy Glasser.

Works Cited

1. Cleveland Clinic. "Gut-Brain Connection," accessed July 28, 2022, https://my.clevelandclinic.org/health/treatments/16358-gut-brain-connection

2. John's Hopkins Medicine. "The Brain-Gut Connection," accessed July 28th, 2022, https://www.hopkinsmedicine.org/health/wellness-and-prevention/the-brain-gut-connection

3. Nikhil Swaminathan, "Why Does the Brain Need So Much Power?" *Scientific American*, April 29, 2008, https://www.scientificamerican.com/article/why-does-the-brain-need-s/

4. Fernando Gomez-Pinilla, "Brain Foods: The Effects of Nutrients on Brain Function," *Nature Reviews Neuroscience*, July 9, 2008, https://www.ncbi.nlm.nih.gov/pmc/articles/PMC2805706/

5. Miles Berger, John A. Gray, and Bryan L. Roth. "The Expanded Biology of Serotonin," *Annu Rev Med*, 2009, https://www.ncbi.nlm.nih.gov/pmc/articles/PMC5864293/

6. Dr. Siri Carpenter, "That Gut Feeling," American Psychological Association, September 2012, https://www.apa.org/monitor/2012/09/gut-feeling

7. The Mayo Clinic. "Selective Serotonin Reuptake Inhibitors (SSRIs)," accessed July 28th, 2022, https://www.mayoclinic.org/diseases-conditions/depression/in-depth/ssris/art-20044825

8. The Stanford Encyclopedia of Philosophy. "William of Ockham," Mar 5, 2019, https://plato.stanford.edu/entries/ockham/

9. Carnegie Melon University. "How stress influences disease: Study reveals inflammation as the culprit," April 2, 2012, https://www.sciencedaily.com/releases/2012/04/120402162546.htm

10. The Mayo Clinic. "Chronic stress puts your health at risk," accessed July 28th, 2022, https://www.mayoclinic.org/healthy-lifestyle/stress-management/in-depth/stress/art-20046037